In the loop

KNITTING NOW

JESSICA HEMMINGS

black dog
publishing
london uk

CON

NTENTS

6 INTRODUCTION / Jessica Hemmings

RETHINKING KNITTING
8

10 Twists, Knots and Holes: Collecting, the Gaze & Knitting the Impossible / Clio Padovani & Paul Whittaker

18 The Perfect / Freddie Robins

24 Flying Kites and Knitting in Public / Sabrina Gschwandtner

26 Knitting has an Image Problem / Linda Newington

NARRATIVE KNITS
32

34 'The Flow of Action': Knitting, Making and Thinking / Mary M Brooks

40 Spinning Straw into Gold: The 'New' Woman in Contemporary Knit Lit / Jo Turney

46 Alter Egos / Mark Newport

56 Finding Your Way Home / Jeanette Sendler

62 Knitting in Southern African Fiction / Jessica Hemmings

SITE AND SIGHT: ACTIVIST KNITTING
66

68 Textiles and Activism / Kirsty Robertson

80 Quiet Activism / Deirdre Nelson

90 Knitting Nation / Liz Collins

96 Threat in the Landscape? / Sophie Horton

106 Encountering 'The Bogey': The Separate—But—Parallel (and non-Mercenary) Cults of Craftivism and Unsentimental Wanton Sexuality, Post-2001 / Lycia Trouton

112 Craft, Queerness, and Guerilla Tactics: An Extended Maker's Statement / Lacey Jane Roberts

PROGRESS: LOOKING BACK
118

120 Knitting Technology comes Full Circle / Sandy Black

128 Looking Backwards to Look Forwards / Annie Shaw

132 Keep & Share / Amy Twigger Holroyd

140 Tracking Knitting and Translating Code / Rachel Beth Egenhoefer

AFTERWORDS
150

150 End Notes

154 Contributor Biographies

157 Acknowledgements

INTROD

JESSICA HEMMINGS

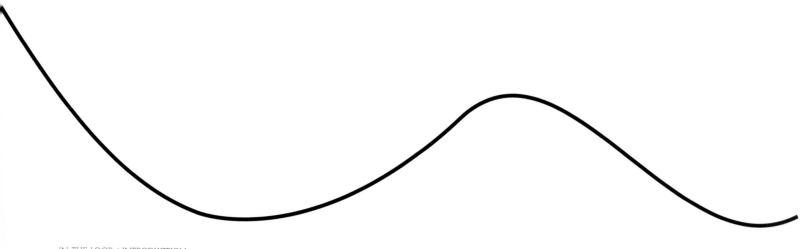

The content of this book originates from the In the Loop conference Linda Newington and I organised at the Winchester School of Art, University of Southampton, in July of 2008. Our interest in organising the conference grew out of the curious and contradictory energy felt around the surge of public interest in knitting we were witnessing. On the one hand, picking up needles and wool are seen as admirable pastimes again; but simultaneously, taking shape is a far more challenging dialogue about the meaning and potential of knitting.

When compiling this book I wanted to avoid at all costs the common pitfall of commentary that speaks only from the perspective of history and theory and erases the voice of the artist and maker along the way. As a result, the contributors to this book have written and illustrated from a number of perspectives and borrow from a variety of conventions. Some provide rich images accompanied by brief statements. Others have elected to write at length about their practice, using the format of the illustrated essay to move equally between word and image. At the opposite extreme are essays that consider knitting in fiction and address the identity of knitting as it appears in print.

Inside this range of formats are an equally diverse variety of voices. Academic, artist, conservator, historian, librarian and poet are all to be found on these pages. There is no chronology at play in the book's organisation and I suggest readers dip and skip to the images and voices that speak to them. I acknowledge that this approach results in a format that strays from what we are conditioned to expect of books: pages of neatly ordered text punctuated at regular intervals with pretty pictures. But it is my hope that this variety introduces a broader range of readers to knitting's diverse endeavours.

Where voices do jar, it is worth asking what they jar against? If this new identity of knitting is unsettling, what exactly was knitting expected to be? I hope, at the very least, that the material contained within these pages provokes dialogue and debate that may contribute to a more broadly considered definition of knitting in the future.

RETHINK
KNITT

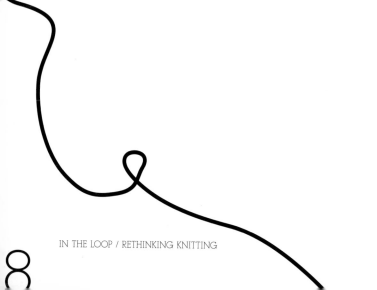

ING
ING

The resurgence of interest knitting enjoys today is not driven by the same motivations that shaped the popularity of knitting in the past. With our practical need for knitting long gone, this popular pastime now appears in unexpected guises with intentions and meanings that stray far outside the realm of the domestic and utilitarian.

Clio Padovani and Paul Whittaker unsettle the benign identity of knitting in their discussion of the photographic images by Margi Geerlinks, which they suggest can be understood as a type of accumulation or collection. Padovani and Whittaker observe the knitted shape in the act of psychoanalysis as well as the zoetrope-like installations of Louise Bourgeois, which force the viewer to circle around the exterior and peer inwards. Throughout their essay, knitting is revealed to be a significant tool for the structuring of both thinking and making.

Freddie Robins pulls apart the image of knitting as a soothing pastime and reveals the tension between perfection and production that guides her use of industrial knitting. Her poetic and forthright account of the aspirations and impossibilities of her practice are illustrated in the *Imperfect* series, garments that do not cover the body, but instead are bodies. These claustrophobic creations are quite unlike a knitted garment that warms. Instead Robins proposes another version of the impossible: textiles that provide no entrance for the wearer, no invitation for the body to inhabit.

Sabrina Gschwandtner takes us, for a moment, away from the grounded world of making. Using the humble thread as her starting point, she offers us a comparison of recreational knitters and the hobby of creating portraits using Kite Arial Photography—KAP. Gschwandtner notes the "sentimental, nostalgic and somewhat sad longing for a stable sense of human scale", which these enigmatic images provide, and links these feelings to the sentiments that drive our current enthusiasm for knitting. In both cases, the virtual web of the internet is central to the new communities kite flyers and knitters use to navigate the social landscape of today.

The final contribution of this section returns to the act of collecting with Linda Newington's frank account of the perception of knitting—fascination and ridicule in equal measure. The Knitting Collection held by the University of Southampton Library preserves the legacy of three distinct collections for public use and reveals what could be understood as yet another 'expanded' definition of knitting. Here we see curious knitted objects alongside ephemeral and tangential records such as patterns.

In each of the contributions to this section, knitting is 'rethought'. Our expectations and assumptions are unsettled and new ways of defining and understanding knitting are proposed. These contributors speak and make from perspectives that teeter on the edges of what we may comfortably understand as knitting today. From these new and slightly precarious positions, they ask us to reconsider what we thought we knew knitting to be.

TWISTS, KNOTS & HOLES: COLLECTING, THE GAZE & KNITTING THE IMPOSSIBLE

CLIO PADOVANI & PAUL WHITTAKER

This essay comes in two parts. The first part proposes an elaboration in thinking about what we have come to know as the act of knitting: an extension in our understanding of the taxonomy of knitting and its categories. The second part aims to expose what might be at stake in an extended definition of contemporary art that unconventionally makes use of the practices of knitting.

Knitting is now a medium and even a reference of choice for many contemporary artists. By way of illustration, Rosemary Trockel has employed the knitted sign, Louise Unger has sculpted body-like forms through the knitting of steel wire and Mike Kelly has used knitted toys in his performances. That said, the work of these artists and others like them, contrasts strongly with the longstanding domestic traditions of knitting. Margi Geerlinks' photograph of a woman holding knitting needles, from which hangs the half finished knitted body of a young girl, exemplifies well this point. Dressed in white, the transfixed woman stares out from the photograph, while a thread of wool snakes down from the knitted body and pools into a ball on the floor. The pictorial alliance of a woman, child and the practice of knitting might conventionally suggest a content of motherhood and the familial. In this image however, these alliances, arranged around the partial form of the knitted body, appear not familial but monstrous. The act of creation, rendered inert by the photograph, appears here more self-driven than a selfless act of life giving: more Dr Frankenstein than a Madonna and child.

If we accept that Geerlinks' photograph is by virtue of content and reference worthy of classification in the codex of knitting, we also accept that by merging art and craft, concept and function, this work and others like it, challenge the convention of knitting. These works transform our understanding of knitting by making knitting more than a practice of knots and loops of thread: they promote the question, what is it to knit?

Susan Stewart offers a key to how we might address this challenge to the taxonomy of knitting. In *On Longing*, Stewart considers how objects collected and stored in museums, whether public or private, mediate experience in time and space. For Stewart, such objects engender interest because "when objects are defined in terms of their use value, they serve as extensions of the body into the environment, but when objects are defined by the collection, such an extension is inverted, so the environment is subsumed into the scenario of the personal."[1] The implication in Stewart's thinking is that collections are constructions or compositions, and that "the ultimate term in the series that marks the collection is the 'self', the articulation of the collector's own 'identity'."[2]

If we follow Stewart's lead we may hypothesise that the components that make up Geerlinks' composed image—the photograph, the background, the posed figure, selected attire, knitted form and the spool of wool—offer the possibility that knitting, for Geerlinks, supplements more than the composition of an image. What Geerlinks can be construed to have done, according to Stewart's thinking, is collected and composed with parts or signifiers, including a knitted object, so as to communicate her message; like a three-dimensional textile, she has knitted together, in time and space, personally significant objects, and organised those conceptual, sometimes literal threads necessary to promote her ideas. In doing so, she has proposed an emergent narrative and herself as a significant term in the collection: the maker, or knitter, of monstrous tales. Geerlinks' image, elaborated by way of Stewart's model, proposes that what we have come to know as the act of knitting might reasonably include the practice of collecting; knitting as the collection and construction of narratives—narratives in which the artist is a primary factor, but not always, necessarily, the creator of disturbing tales.

If we can rethink and extend the process of knitting to include the practice of collecting, what might be at stake in an art that knits by way of collecting; art that unconventionally explores the boundaries of the knotting and looping of threads?

Louise Bourgeois is a prolific artist known for her intense psychologically driven sculptures, installations and drawings. Her work draws upon her childhood memories and the complex emotions involved in familial relationships. The Daros Collection of Bourgeois drawings completed between 1994–1995, published under the title *The Insomnia Drawings*, offers a number of images that interestingly represent and reference the making of a textile. Take for example, *Le Cauchemar de Hayter*, an ink on lined paper drawing. This drawing does not appear to be a representation of a particular object but instead suggests, through its overlapped meandering lines with peaks and troughs, a looped pattern, a kind of knitted doodle.

When considered by way of the writings of Jacques Lacan, Bourgeois' unconventional textiles serve the purpose of suggesting the gaze as a pertinent critical tool through which we might identify and explore what is at stake in an art that knits unconventionally. Referring to the work of Catherine Yass, the psychoanalyst Parveen Adams quotes how Lacan describes, in the process of psychoanalysis, "that which from time makes a stuff of it [what is said] is not borrowed from the imaginary, but rather from a textile, where the knots speak of nothing but the holes which are there".[3] This means that no matter how much material the patient enunciates, there is always something missing in the process of analysis. What is described circles around a hole.

All textiles, even knitted doodles, are composed in part of holes or gaps and this allows both Lacan and Adams to identify the textile as a metaphor for the subject's experience during analysis. The hole around which Lacanian analysis circles is the gaze, and the gaze stands for the object that can never be attained. "It is a [hole] in the subject's seemingly omnipotent look": a gap that "marks the spot at which our desire manifests itself in what we see."[4] The gaze is the cause of desire rather than the object towards which desire tends and as such it is a hole that sets the drives in motion.[5] Fantasy allows the subject to relate to the unattainable gaze or hole by constructing a scene through which we, as subject, can take up a relation to its impossibility.

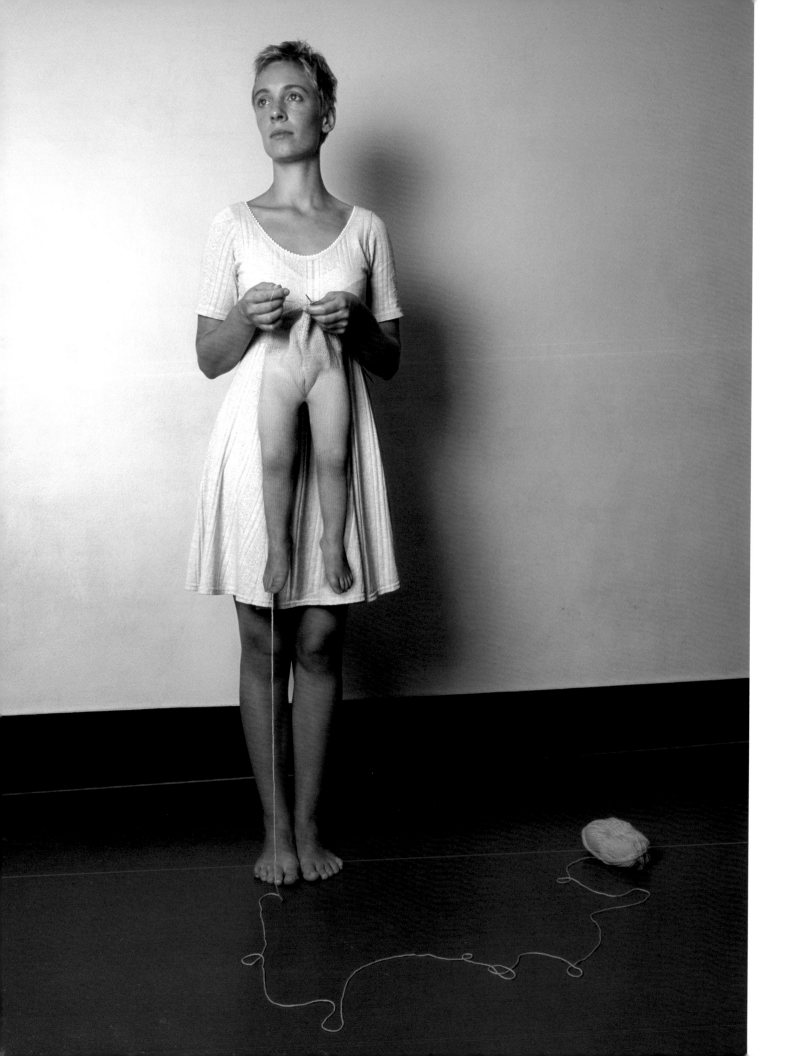

The film theorist Todd McGowan argues that it is the excess in the fantasy image that marks the hole or gap of the gaze and that the excess of the film image may be seen in "unconventional camera work, obtrusive editing, or in the content of the film, when [for example], the dominant story line is unexpectedly interrupted in a surprising or shocking manner".[6] The cinema influences many contemporary artists, and photographic and digital practices utilise much the same means of communication as Hollywood. In the same way that contemporary cinema can be critiqued by way of fantasy stained by the excesses of the gaze, so can, we might argue, contemporary arts which similarly construct a fantasmatic appearance. The compositions of fantasy scenes, whether in film, paint, fabric, knitting or collections, offer an opportunity for narrative interpretation and discussion of the gaze as a concern of making.

Louise Bourgeois' *Red Room (Parents)*, and its companion piece *Red Room (Child)*, both 1994, offer the viewer an installation experience that might very well be described as the fantastic product of a highly suggestive collection and its interwoven narratives. The works constitute two installations of objects housed in two cell or zoetrope-like structures made from old doors. They are experienced by the viewer moving around the apertures between the doors and investigating from different vantage points the objects placed within.

Inside the enclosed space of *Red Room (Parents)* we find an arranged display of a bed and furniture. Yet everything in this room is not as it at first appears. More pertinently, this room appears conditioned by the double. The bed is double, the chests of drawers are double and a large oval mirror doubles the contents yet again. In this world of reflections the bed is made and the pillows are plumped up and ready for use. This is, however, no place of rest. Although orderly, this bed does not lend itself to relaxation. The room is a stage-set for the imaginary action of its occupiers: the absent and imagined parents.

Although similarly installed as a hidden space screened from the viewer, the character and suggestive quality of *Red Room (Child)* is very different. Where the room of the parents is cool, orderly and distant, by virtue of the reflective doubling, the room of the child is comparatively disordered, immediate and compelling. The collected objects, arranged and displayed around the walls, vary in their material but are compelling by virtue of their colourful unity. Key to the scene is an industrial thread stand that holds several spools of red thread. As Rainer Crone and Petrus Graf Schaesberg write:

> If the smoothed out sheet [of the parents bed] is concealing chimeras of hidden desire, lust, and sensual pleasure; if its dense weave is imbued with the complexities of an unrestrained, unbridled imagination; if a solid warp and weft of complicity knots together this sheltered world of conventional, traditional, acceptable sentiments; then the thin, breakable thread in the child's room reveals the unfinished process of creative construction, a loosely-structured world of possibilities.[7]

In these stage-sets for the imagination, from where might instances of the gaze, the excess of vision, look back at us and prompt our desire to know, interpret and fantasise? If we remember Geerlinks' excessive image, here the monstrously deformed red glass hand and forearm, placed in tender proximity to smaller child-like versions, might promote interpretation through the excesses of the body. There are however two other instances of real excess that might properly be considered examples of the gaze; one is formal, the other an unexpected, unexplainable alien interruption to the predominant fantasy scene.[8]

At a formal level the zoetrope-like wooden door structure of both installations offers an excess of vision in two ways. First, the many vertical gaps between each door invite new and different perspectives, although the excess of vantage points reveals only more partial or occluded looking, and does not illuminate previously unseen detail. Secondly, when viewed outside and from a distance, the straining eye of the viewer sees an outside punctuated by many holes; an excess of holes that obscure the external world through the fantasy of the interior.

The alien object that interrupts the interior scene of the installations is the pink rubberised and elongated form, which hangs from a hook on the industrial thread stand. This pink form has a matt sheen and smooth surface, occasionally punctured by long pins. Its form alludes to organic matter and the body. It is excessive because of its infinite capacity to suggest interpretation. This is an object that can be many things and simultaneously nothing. It is suggestive of ham, sexual parts, body limbs, even a bladder. For Lacan, that which drives desire—the gaze, object, the "real"—is outside language and inassimilable to symbolisation. It is that which resists signification because it is impossible to integrate into the symbolic order, and this accounts for its traumatic quality. Based on this definition, Bourgeois' pink rubber intrusion may, through its incomprehensibility, be understood as a truly impossible object.

The aim of this essay was two-fold, to propose an extended taxonomy of knitting and to explore what might be at stake in unconventional contemporary art practices that knot and loop with threads. Susan Stewart's thinking about language and objects has enabled us to propose that more elaborate thinking about the act of knitting might reasonably include knitting as collecting; the collection or composition of diverse objects selected and arranged to promote a narrative thread: a fantasy of the 'self'. The metaphor of the hole in textiles similarly allows us to utilise the Lacanian gaze to critique an example of this extended classification of knitting and establish what might be wagered in such modes of making. From the study of Bourgeois' *Red Room* installations we can speculate that these works offer the risk of an encounter with the gaze. We may conclude, therefore, that in an extended taxonomy of knitting, what is at stake is not only the perpetuation of a self-fantasy but an encounter with the unassimilatable: the impossible.

previous page MARGI GEERLINKS, *Untitled*, 1997–1998. Edition of six each, cibachrome, plexiglass, dibond, 99 x 73.5 cm, 178 x 124.5 cm. Image courtesy TORCH gallery.
right LOUISE BOURGEOIS, *Red Room (Parents)*, 1994. Mixed media, 248 x 427 x 424 cm. Collection Ursula Hauser, Switzerland. Photograph by Peter Bellamy.

LOUISE BOURGEOIS, *Red Room (Child)*, 1994. Mixed media, 211 x 353 x 274.5 cm.
Collection Musée d'Art Contemporain de Montréal. Photograph by Marcus Schneider.

THE PERFECT

FREDDIE ROBINS

"It's not perfect, but who cares?" Well I do. I enjoy imperfection in you and yours, but not in me and mine. I am very attracted to the imperfections, failings, and roughness of the material world. I enjoy the evidence of human hands, the inevitable wear and repair of objects. I love the obviously handmade. But I suffer from being a perfectionist.

This body of work deals with the constant drive for perfection. It is made using technology that was developed to achieve perfection. Technology developed for mass production to make garment multiples that are exactly the same as each other: garments that do not require any hand finishing, garments whose manufacture does not produce any waste, garments whose production does not require the human touch. Garments that are, supposedly, perfect.

The knitted multiples are produced through the use of a Shima Seiki WholeGarment® machine—a computerised, automated, industrial V-bed flat machine, which is capable of knitting a seamless garment. These multiples take the form of life-size, three-dimensional human bodies. They are combined in a variety of different ways to create large-scale sculptures and installations.

The titles for these works take the form of mathematical equations. The titles give my formula for the arrangement of the multiples. This embracing of numbers and mathematics relates to my love of numbers. As a child I was a good mathematician. I loved the way that numbers gave you certainties. The answer was right or wrong, perfect or imperfect.

Perfectionism is associated with good craftsmanship, something to aspire to. I aim for perfection in all aspects of my life, my work and myself. It can be very debilitating and exhausting, it is of course, truly unachievable, and ultimately undesirable.

The Perfect knitted sculpture for public exhibition was funded by the Arts and Humanities Research Council, AHRC, and the Royal College of Art, Research Development Fund.

clockwise from left FREDDIE ROBINS, *The Perfect: Alex*, 2007. Wool and acrylic yarn, 58 x 92 cm, first sample, knitted small-scale to test the knitting programme. Photograph by Damian Chapman; Shima Seiki SWG First. ® 184L WholeGarment® knitting machine; The computer interface for the Shima Seiki SWG First. ® 184L WholeGarment® knitting machine; The bodies are knitted feet first ending with the top of the head. They fall from the machine fully knitted. All that remains to be done is to remove the waste yarn and sew in the ends. Images courtesy the artist.

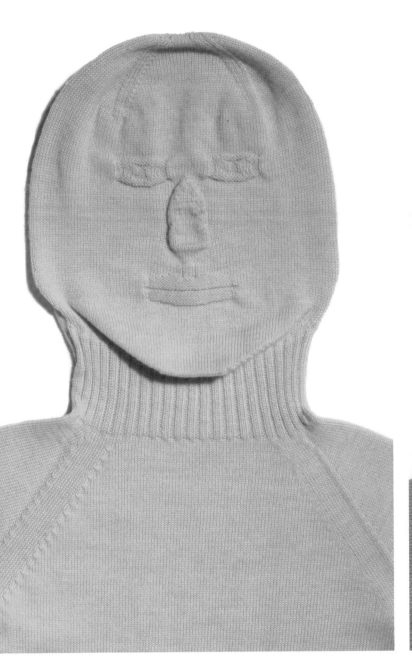

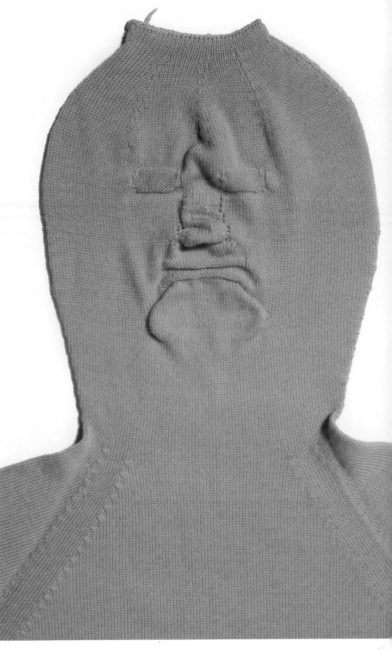

opposite FREDDIE ROBINS, *The Perfect: Tom*, 2007. Wool and acrylic yarn, 36 x 11 cm, fourth sample, knitted small-scale to test a new programme for knitting faces. Photograph Douglas Atfield.

left Final full size sample. Smooth shaping and minimal finish possible with the addition of 2 x 2 rib to give more texture and to achieve shaping for neck and shoulders, achieving a three-dimensional detail in the face whilst maintaining knitted fabric quality through the use of partial knitting—flashage—and interlock—birdseye. Photograph by Douglas Atfield.

right Third sample, first full-size sample. Trying to shape the top of the head without having noticeable fully fashioning marks. It was not possible to get the amount of shaping needed through this method. Trying to achieve three-dimensional detail in the face, whilst maintaining knitted fabric quality. Photograph by Douglas Atfield.

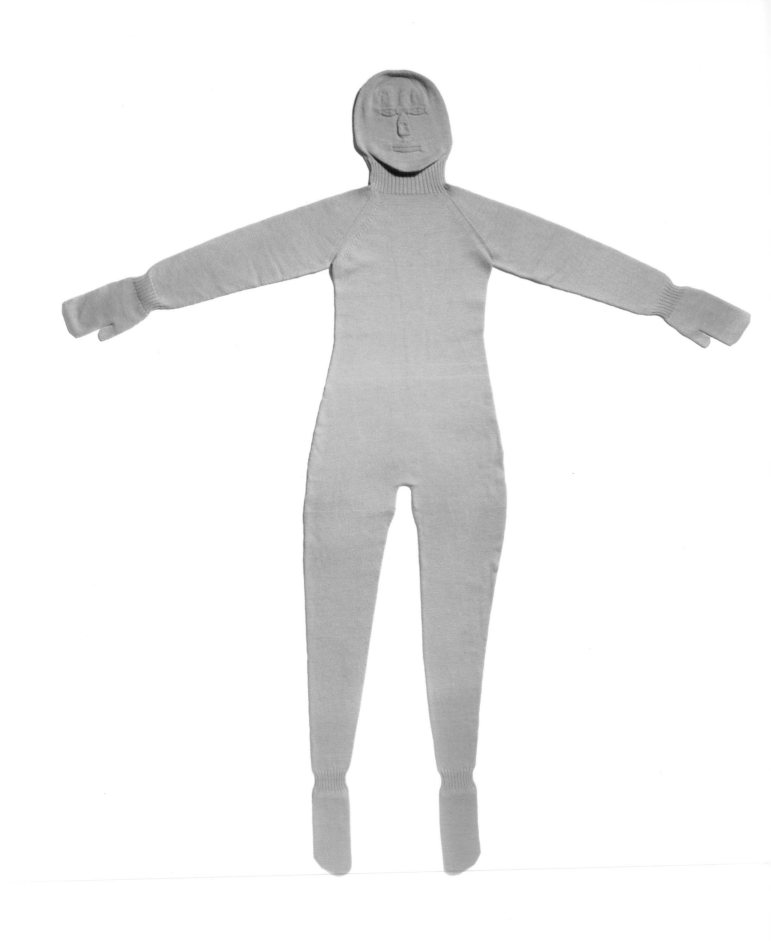

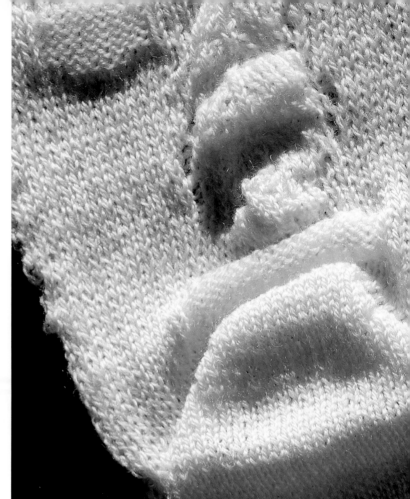

opposite FREDDIE ROBINS, *The Perfect Body*, 2007. Wool yarn, 192 x 164 cm, final full size sample. Photograph by Douglas Atfield.

clockwise from top left Final floor-based installation of knitted bodies and exhibition of models and artefacts. Contemporary Applied Arts, London, 2007. Image courtesy the artist; FREDDIE ROBINS, *The Perfect: Alex* (detail), 2007. Photograph by Damian Chapman; FREDDIE ROBINS, *Self Portrait with The Perfect*, 2007. Portrait after photograph of Katharina Detzel, 1914. Katharina Detzel, (1872—1941), spent 19 years hospitalised in an institution in Klingenmünster, Germany. She made, amongst other objects, a life-size doll from bags and straw. She was a campaigner against social injustice, particularly against women and children. She became a victim of the euthanasia programmes in 1941. Photograph by Celia Pym.

SABRINA GSCHWANDTNER, *KAP* (detail), 2009. Inkjet print on cotton
broadcloth with string, 25.5 x 355.5 cm. Image courtesy the artist and Solo
Impression, Inc.

FLYING KITES AND KNITTING

SABRINA GSCHWANDTNER

Five years ago, just clicking around online, I discovered Kite Aerial Photography. KAP is done by hobby photographers who tie their cameras to kites in order to take low-level aerial shots. Most KAP enthusiasts photograph spaces close to home, like their backyards and local parks.

I started collecting KAP self-portraits; the ones taken from odd angles as the wind forced the kite back down toward its caretaker. In these shots, the kite string ties the tiny, grounded photographer to a space above, beyond the photograph's borders.

When Solo Impression print studio founder, Judith Solodkin, suggested that we work together on a project, I knew that I wanted to work with these photos. I decided to print a group of them on a length of fabric and then tie them all together into three-dimensional space. I sewed thread from the spot where the string in each photograph ended, and connected those threads to hooks installed on a wall. The result was a ten-foot print anchored at various points, resembling a kite or a pinned insect specimen.

When I look at the piece, I vicariously experience that peculiar pleasure that comes from seeing and locating oneself as a small object in a vast landscape. I feel a sentimental, nostalgic and somewhat sad longing for a stable sense of human scale. I see a desire for community, and for a connection, perhaps celestial, beyond one's locality.

As a knitter, I recognise in KAP a similar way of working—not just with hands, string, solitude, and meditative craft, but also with the internet. Knitters and KAPers both have very active online lives. They blog, share technical resources on specialised forums, and create galleries of their work. The online personas of these crafts are becoming just as important as the crafts themselves.

Many KAPers say the advent of the internet helped their hobby become popular, and knitters say that too. It's a complicated relationship: in reaction to the speed and disembodiment of internet connectivity, people turn to handcraft for slowness, corporeality and tactility. Then they turn back to the internet to re-connect. We're navigating a circular route from material to immaterial, using string or yarn to test what's within our reach.

KNITTING HAS AN IMAGE PROBLEM

LINDA NEWINGTON

Knitting has an image problem. The word is often met with an impassioned response, but that passion is not always positive. Recognition of the diversity and variety of ways that knitting can be approached and understood is key to dismantling the narrow and somewhat blinkered responses the vast discipline of knitting sometimes encounters. The Knitting Collections held by the University of Southampton Library reveal an image of knitting at its most eclectic, charting the nostalgic and the kitsch, alongside the elegant and pedestrian.

The interests and commitment of three individuals, Montse Stanley, Richard Rutt, and Jane Waller, have shaped the collection in very different ways. Each has brought a distinctive approach to the act of collecting and contributes a unique perspective to our current understanding of knitting. The result is a collection that enjoys an identity which extends beyond the obvious.

Montse Stanley, (1942–1999), was born in Barcelona and established her collection as the Knitting Reference Library in her Cambridge home before its acquisition by the University in 1999. Her collecting started in a modest way with historic postcards and photographs on the theme of knitting, acquired while attending postcard fairs with her husband, Thomas Stanley, who possessed one of the largest postcard businesses in the country. Also part of the collection are over eight hundred knitted objects, many influenced by her Spanish birthplace.

In recognition of his long standing knitting friendship with Montse Stanley, Richard Rutt, popularly known as the "Knitting Bishop" generously donated his library to the University in 2000. A particular feature of this collection are a number of Victorian knitting books first printed for wide distribution in the 1830s. These groundbreaking books represent a translation of handcraft practice into written and visual form. Several thousand knitting patterns, with an otherwise often overlooked emphasis on menswear, are also part of this collection. These patterns record not only the recent technical history of knitting, but also offer a glimpse of past popular culture and graphic design.

Jane Waller is known for her pioneering design work with vintage knitting patterns. Her collection of five thousand patterns, which she discovered by chance during a house clearance, along with her published books, are also part of the collection. Today this material reflects the popularity hand knitting enjoyed in its cyclical revivals throughout the past century and into the present.

The Knitting Collections held at the University of Southampton Library bring together these three distinct collections for public use. Although each collection is individual in nature, together this material reminds us of knitting's seldom appreciated diversity.

top Eighteenth century beaded bag (detail). Montse Stanley Collection. Photograph by Mike Halliwell. Courtesy the University of Southampton Library.

bottom Twentieth century beaded bag (detail). Montse Stanley Collection. Photograph by Mike Halliwell. Courtesy the University of Southampton Library.

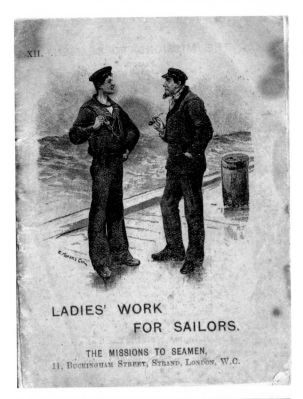

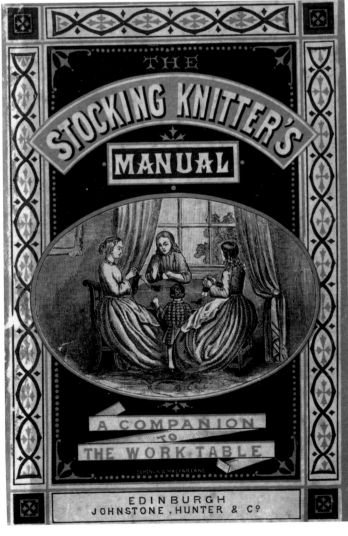

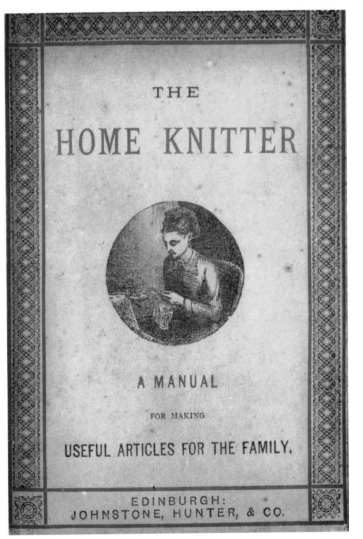

opposite Poodle. Montse Stanley Collection. Photograph by Mike Halliwell. Courtesy the University of Southampton Library.

top *Ladies Work for Sailors*, circa 1800. Richard Rutt Library. Courtesy the University of Southampton Library.

bottom left *The Stocking Knitter's Manual: A Companion to the Worktable*, circa 1870. Richard Rutt Library. Courtesy the University of Southampton Library.

bottom right *The Home Knitter: A Manual for Making Useful Articles for the Family*, 1876. Richard Rutt Library. Courtesy the University of Southampton Library.

top Bumble bees. Montse Stanley Collection. Photograph by Mike Halliwell. Courtesy of the University of Southampton Library.
bottom Elephants. Montse Stanley Collection. Photograph by Mike Halliwell. Courtesy of the University of Southampton Library.
opposite Dolly tea cosy. Montse Stanley Collection. Photograph by Mike Halliwell. Courtesy of the University of Southampton Library.

NARRA
K

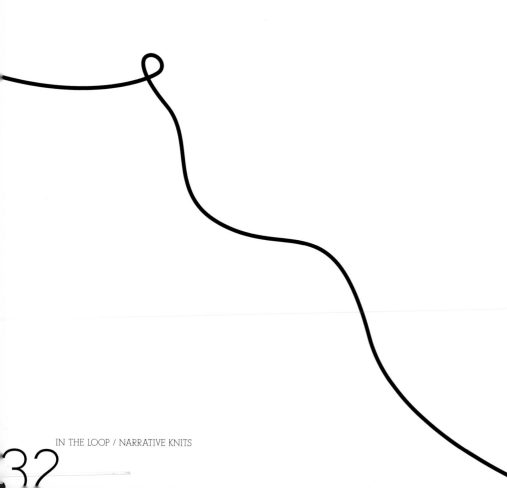

TIVE NITS

Knitting appears in written and oral narrative traditions, from cultures with a lengthy history of the craft, such as the Scottish Islands of Shetland, as well as those with an imported history of knitting, such as Zimbabwe. Curiously knitting is not, as we might expect, always cast in a positive light when it appears in fiction and folklore. It is as often used to navigate grief, disappointment or loss, as it does a romantic return to the soothing rhythms of working with our hands.

Mary Brooks describes her anguished attempts as a child not when learning to read, but when learning to knit. From this sympathetic position of a frustrated knitter, Brooks considers literature in which knitting is not always the source of comfort or solace, but is the reason for irritation, anxiety and disappointment. Rather than literary theory, Brooks reads her literary references with an eye for where textual evidence meets archival objects and is substantiated by personal experience.

Jo Turney introduces us to recent popular literature in which knitting "acts as a barometer of female morality". Drawing on recent examples of fiction that borrow from the genres of murder mystery and romance novels, Turney exposes the central, but often contradictory position of knitting that provides partial empowerment for female protagonists. Many of these narratives reek of cliché and Turney notes that the absence of "gritty realism that is the preserve of the male detective" throws into question the ability of this fiction to fundamentally change not only the identity of knitting, but the role of women in patriarchal society.

Mark Newport uses knitting to challenge the super hero narratives that informed his "childhood memories of the ultimate man". The acrylic full body suits he knits and wears in staged photographs mock the bravado of these characters, while testing our own acceptance of knitting found beyond the zones in which it has long been tethered. In contrast to Freddie Robins machine knit bodies, Newport knits by hand, using his choice of yarn and colour, guided by childhood memories. Hidden under the considerable humour is a more serious commentary based on Newport's "realisation that when someone sees me knitting there is often a comment that acknowledges that a man knitting is exceptional in some way".

Jeanette Sendler's series of large-scale knitted installations made from Shetland wool are inspired by the folklore of the northern Scottish islands. In stark contrast to the hurried time Turney observes contemporary women snatching for their knitting, Sendler reflects on an earlier era when the wives of fishermen would use the amount of knitting they had completed to gauge the amount of time the men had been at sea. Constructing large scalloped shapes suggestive of the strong currents around the Shetland Islands, Sendler translates evocative oral narratives back into the original materials of the region. Her visual representations of these narratives capture, to use her words, "the innate, internal rhythms employed by the women to measure their men folk's return".

The final contribution to this section looks beyond the European literary traditions on our doorstep for evidence of the knitted artefact. Recent fiction by authors from southern Africa, a region whose literary heritage is founded on the oral tradition, often constructs unique narrative voices that use the beguiling technique of unreliable narration. Here I note that knitting is initially deployed to lull readers into a false sense of security, before redeploying the craft to speak of unexpected, at times even unspeakable, themes.

While the idea that knitting is linked to storytelling is far from new, the examples of narratives containing reference to knitting discussed in this section reveal unexpected perspectives. Because we associate knitting with positive and achievable activities, it is a theme ripe for reworking both by contemporary fiction authors, as well as artists, such as Sendler and Newport, who use narrative as a core element of their studio practice.

'THE FLOW OF ACTION': KNITTING, MAKING AND THINKING

MARY M BROOKS

I cannot remember learning to read. For me, a lucky child, black marks on white paper rapidly distinguished themselves and became an entry into a world of make-believe and exploration. But I do remember learning to knit. I remember sitting hunched up, striving to manipulate long, too long, slippery needles and laboriously struggling to loop recalcitrant wool on and off those blunt points. My knitting never grew in neat rows; it was distorted and full of runs and dropped stitches. I remember feeling that I was failing some test, a test my mother and my grandmother effortlessly passed as they produced itchy jumpers, socks made on four needles and, more thrilling, miniature dolls' clothes.

Knitting historians, such as Richard Rutt and Montse Stanley, amongst others, have built the foundation for scholarly understanding of knitting history and technology, but memories such as mine of making, and failing to make, knitting seem to have been little discussed.[1] This essay is therefore a preliminary attempt to use models developed by archaeologists and social anthropologists to explore making and the made. It uses ideas of gesture and manipulation to explore the relationship between the surviving knitted artefact and what it can—and cannot—indicate about the practice and experience of making knitting.

KNITTING AS ARTEFACT AND PRACTICE

The English language fuses both the activity of knitting: "I am knitting", with the resulting made artefact: "my knitting". While the techniques and the resulting textile structure are one linguistically, the knitted artefacts are the sole surviving physical evidence of an activity, which took place in the past. As such, they contain evidence which enables us to reconstruct the techniques—in this case manipulation of thread and needles—employed by the maker. Sometimes only those who understand current practice can help to understand past methods. I vividly remember learning from the animated discussion of a group of skilled knitters how a collection of small Victorian knitted 'pence jugs' had been made. This is an area where contemporaneous textual evidence fails us. Rutt lists the Victorian knitting books, which describe methods for making pence jugs but notes that such instructions are often "impossible to follow or contain alarming mistakes".[2] The makers' knowledge and embodied skill enabled them to 'unpick' mentally the evidence of making from the made artefacts.

The existence of knitting implies the skilled and repetitive manipulation of tools, albeit deceptively simple tools, in the case of knitting needles. The social anthropologist Tim Ingold argued that the making of tools implies a chain of planned and interlocking actions and exchanges: "The tool-using skills of contemporary human beings are embedded in a social process of cooperative production that presupposes role complementarity, the social exchange of tools and materials...."[3] The use of tools also implies the existence of skills and techniques, which are not just the mechanical application of external forces but also involve care, judgement and dexterity in "attentive" engagement.[4] Memory of the correct order in which knitting needles are to be manipulated to make simple or complex stitches in the right order, and judgement of the correct design is necessary to produce a knitted artefact, which conforms to socially defined norms, whether this is a hat, a jumper or a bedspread.

Gibson has observed "speech and gesture do not fossilize"; the objects created by gesture are the surviving evidence of the gesture itself.[5] However, although knitted artefacts are invaluable in understanding the outcome of practice they are limited in the degree and exactitude of the evidence of gesture they reveal. Can knitted artefacts tell us exactly how the knitter held the needles, how he or she moved their hands, how they learnt to remember the correct order in which to manipulate yarn and needles, or what they thought about the knitting? Sometimes flaws in the knitting can provide some evidence about the state of mind or the health of the maker. My own overly tight knitting revealed only too clearly the anxiety I experienced in its making, and the excess tension, which I transmitted through the needles and yarn into the knitted fabric. Dropped stitches, which she had helped to pick up again, enabled the then Duchess of York to identify a knitted scarf worn by a man in a welcoming crowd as one made by the ailing Queen Victoria: "Your scarf must be one of the six scarves... which the dear Queen was knitting before she died. They were her last pieces of work."[6]

LEARNING TO KNIT

Although hand knitting has clearly had an important domestic and economic history until the recent outpourings on the internet, few knitters have written about the pleasures of knitting and even fewer have written about the varied tyrannies of knitting or learning to knit.[7] Literary references therefore gain particular significance in reinforcing, or contradicting, such recent oral evidence for personal experiences.

Learning to knit is a vivid memory for many, whether pleasant or unpleasant. Ingold describes the learning of skill as:

a purposeful alignment of the novice's attention to the movements of others, and a coordination of that attention with the novice's own movements so as to achieve a purposeful alignment of the kind of rhythmic adjustment or resonance that is the hallmark of fluent performance....[8]

In short, this is an intense, one-to-one experience of learning, a relationship of "body, gesture and artefact [in] a process of an intimate interaction".[9] Although sentimentalised by Victorian artists such as Hugh Carter, such experiences of learning to knit can function not just as a transmission of knowledge and skill but also of femininity and familial love across the generations:

I was first taught to knit in school at about age seven, but did not learn how until my granny took those squeaky sweat stained pins, and those tighter than tight knots alternating with holes and said 'enough'. In between pancakes and waspy jam, she showed me the magic of 'in, over, through, and off', making loose string dishcloths in good old garter stitch, then graduating to a scarf. I remember sitting with my granny when I was about 13, and the calming effect of knitting a fuzzy blue twinset for my hormonal nonsense with the familiarity of row after row for my drowsy gran.[10]

Many women memorialise this emotional experience by preserving knitting needles and knitting bags belonging to their mothers and aunts, whether they retain or practice the skill of knitting. Even now, few European and North American women, possibly responding to long ingrained social codes and definitions of femininity, confess to hating

to knit or failing to learn to knit. The negative experience of this twenty-first century woman was, interestingly, divorced from the family context: "My family didn't knit. I once tried as a child but by the seventh red and white stripe on my attempted scarf, I was ready to eat sprouts rather than continue."[11]

This definition of what makes a knitting method 'correct' is, of course, culturally defined. Elizabeth Zimmermann, a renowned American knitter, learned to knit first from her mother and aunts in the English style, and later from her Swiss governess in the Continental Style and, in turn, taught her daughter.[12] Both methods produced knitted artefacts which appear the same, but which were created according to different 'correct' methods. These differences in making persist and can both separate and connect knitters, the technique sometimes superseding the need for language. I remember a long Italian train journey with an English friend, a skilled knitter who was diverting herself from delays and missed connections by knitting a jumper requiring complex stitches and shaping. We were joined in our carriage by a group of elderly black-dressed Italian ladies. They were intrigued by the alien knitting method. An animated discussion ensued, crossing the boundaries of age, language and culture, knitters from different traditions contending that their different methods of manipulating the needles and moving the hands and arms were 'correct'. This is a nice example of Ingold's contention that:

> what the practitioner does to things is grounded in an active perceptual involvement with them. This involvement underwrites the qualities of care, judgement, and dexterity that are of the essence of skilled workmanship… the practitioner's engagement with the material is an attentive engagement rather than a mere mechanical coupling—because he [sic] watches, listens and feels as he works.[13]

KNITTING AND THE BODY

Hand knitting self-evidently involves movements of fingers, hands and arms, together with bodily control in terms of posture. Marcel Mauss, a French sociologist and anthropologist, characterised such control as "techniques of the body". Mauss argued such embodied meaningfulness involving a "novel sequence of movements" may also "presuppose an instrument."[14] In this case, the instrument is the knitting needle. These may be seen as extensions of the fingers and hands, which may also be used successfully on their own in the technique known as 'finger knitting'. The use of needles however enables wider and heavier pieces of knitting to be created and manipulated. For a skilled knitter, the needle becomes part of the hand in a process of motion and making, which Ingold describes almost poetically: "In the flow of action, the body itself becomes transparent, as do the tools attached to it, which—like the body—are as much a part of the user as they are used."[15]

opposite Pence Jug, knitted red, grey and black wool. Montse Stanley collection MS 332 50/11/6. Courtesy the University of Southampton Library.
right Knitting sheaths. Montse Stanley collection MS 332/55. Courtesy the University of Southampton Library.

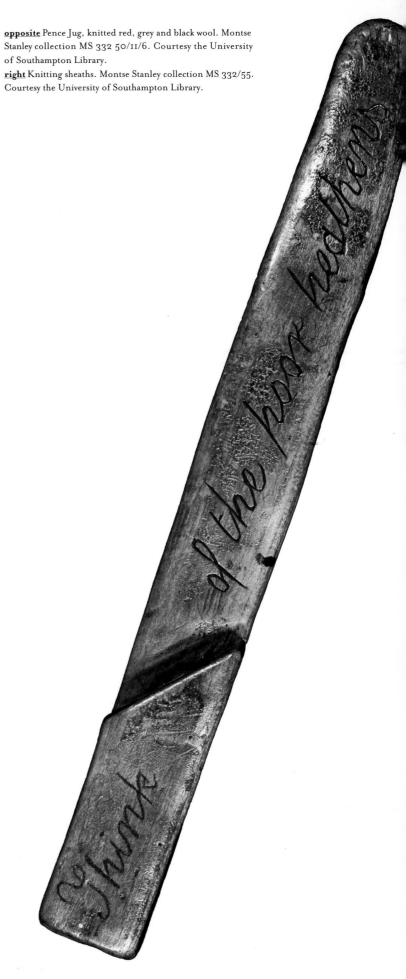

Compare this with Howitt's description of Mrs Crabtree, a twentieth century knitter from Dent, a north English town renowned for its knitting tradition:

> The secret of the method is the rhythmic up and down movement of the arms, performed so the right needle 'strikes the loop' without the least hesitation. The body sways up and down with this action, which is something like the beating of a drum. It is impossible to do it in slow motion and the loops fly off quicker than the eye can see.[16]

Although the interpretation of this repetitive action is contested, the point here is the animation—"the flow of action". The body as well as the hands is involved in the act of knitting. In some knitting traditions, such as Portugal, Peru and the Balkans, the yarn is tensioned by passing it around the neck. The whole body and its physical positioning in space is thus part of the action of knitting.[17] The body can also be physically extended through the use of knitting sheaths, which were made in a variety of materials and forms. Their function was to fix the right-hand needle in position so only the left-hand needle needed manipulation, thus speeding up the knitting process and reducing physical stress. Their role as a bodily extension and modification is further emphasised by Victorian concerns over the impact of their use on posture and health.[18]

IDEAS OF DIFFERENCE IN MEN'S AND WOMEN'S KNITTING

Matthews' argument about the specificity of gesture in terms of gender and class illuminates understanding of the ways in which different techniques of handling knitting needles are understood: "Gestures are often culturally and socially exclusive, and as well as representing significant differences between societies, they also differentiate between groups within societies, such as across age, gender and status."[19] Rutt goes to considerable pains to distinguish what he terms "drawing room knitting" from that of English working, and working class, knitters. The latter held the right-hand needle under the palm, whereas polite ladies held the needle elegantly like a pen to display their gentility and refinement: "no feminine employment is better calculated to display a pretty hand and graceful motions than knitting".[20] The "polite" style of knitting became dominant despite its relative inefficiency.[21] Ibsen's use of knitting as an indicator of status in his play *The Doll's House* thus becomes much more pointed. Helmer's critique of Mrs Linde's knitting method is not only an attack on her unbecoming gestures, which reveal her lower class status, but also on her lack of femininity:

> Helmer   So you knit?
> Mrs Linde   Of course.
> Helmer   Do you know, you ought to embroider.
> Mrs Linde   Really? Why?
> Helmer   Yes, it's far more becoming. Let me show you. You hold the embroidery thus in your left hand, and use the needle with the right—like this—with a long, easy sweep. Do you see?
> Mrs Linde   Yes, perhaps—
> Helmer   But in the case of knitting—that can never be anything but ungraceful; look here—the arms close together, the knitting—needles going up and down—it has a sort of Chinese effect.[22]

Significantly, some writers have argued that men have a fundamentally different method of knitting:

> Men have always been great knitters, and hold their own particular ideas on the subject, which differ considerably from the style of knitting today. Sailors… often form their knitting stitches in a different way from women, hold their needles, which they prefer to be of strong steel, flat in both hands and generally knit with the yarn in the left hand.[23]

Using a different knitting gesture signifies that the male is not giving in to the dominance of the female associations of knitting.

KNITTING VERSUS THINKING

Exploring how knitting is positioned in opposition, both as part of female learning, and in opposition to female thinking, is revealing. As well as being a necessary domestic skill, knitting has long formed part of girls' formal education. Seventeenth century charity schools taught their girls knitting, sewing and spinning rather than reading. Although this could provide them with a livelihood, it also reduced their educational scope. As late as 1915, knitting still formed part of private education at home for upper class girls. The rigorous timetable followed by Elizabeth Alington, later wife of the British Prime Minster Alex Douglas-Home, is evidence of this:

> Elizabeth's timetable… when she was six, began at 8.40 am and finished at 4.40 pm, Monday to Saturday. It included Naturework, Music, Knitting, Number, Composition, History/Story, Phonetics, Poetry, Geography, French, Expression Work, Composition, Dictation, Copy, Reading and Handwork….[24]

Note that knitting comes before mathematics, French and reading. The spirit in which knitting was undertaken was also significant. Antonia White records how her heroine and alter ego, the schoolgirl Nanda, was told by the nuns that it was better to knit socks humbly for the glory of God rather than write the finest poem or symphony for self glorification.[25] Knitting may also be used as a symbol for intellectual failure. Dorothy L Sayers is most famous for her fictional detective Lord Peter Whimsy, but her novels also explore women's roles and argue for women's right to an intellectual life. In the novel *Thrones, Dominations*, Harriet Vane, Lord Peter's wife, herself the author of detective novels, is described as having difficulty writing following her marriage into a different class. Harriet's lack of creative production is compared to her secretary's knitting, which grows in inverse proportion to Harriet's novel: "Miss Bracy the secretary sat before the silent typewriter, reproachfully knitting a jumper. Miss Bracy always looked reproachful when there was no manuscript for her to get on with...."[26]

CONCLUSION

The aim of this essay was to use ideas about gesture and practice, to open up alternative routes by which the skill of knitting may be examined and valued. Analysis of gesture, manipulation and bodily posture developed in other disciplines, may enrich thinking about the practice, which created the knitted artefacts. It is hoped that, rather than offending knitters, archaeologists and anthropologists alike, it will lay the foundation for further debate about the personal and social value and meaning of knitting.

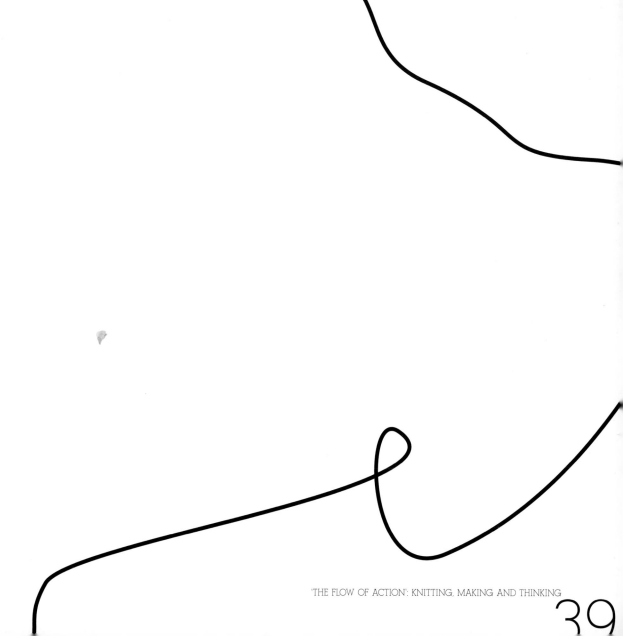

SPINNING STRAW INTO GOLD: THE 'NEW' WOMAN IN CONTEMPORARY KNIT LIT

JO TURNEY

Caught between life, love and pursuit of the perfect cast-on, these three friends learnt that there are never any easy answer, except maybe one—when the going gets tough, the tough get knitting.[1]

The inclusion of knitting in fiction about, and for women, has a history that dates back to the eighteenth century. Jane Austen, for example, describes knitting for pleasure and charity in *Persuasion*. Since this time, knitting has featured within the novels of Virginia Woolf—*Jacob's Room*; AS Byatt—*Art Work*, *The Matisse Stories*; and Edith Wharton—*Roman Fever and Other Stories*, to name but a few. Rarely though has knitting been more than a sub-text, as with characters such as Agatha Christie's Miss Marple and Patricia Wentworth's Miss Silver; or metaphor, Daphné du Maurier's *Rebecca*; or merely an occupation that enables characters to busy their hands, appear invisible, or demonstrate their feminine characteristics—Dorothy L Sayers' *Lord Peter Wimsey Mysteries*. Indeed, the iconology of the knitting woman, as outlined in fiction, can be understood as an allegory for femininity and the wiles of womanhood, through attributes such as innocuousness, diligence, thrift, handwork and storytelling.

Since the 1990s, the characterisation of the knitting woman has developed to such an extent that she has become the protagonist in a new genre of fiction aimed at a female readership: Knit Lit. Capitalising on a revival of interest in knitting as demonstrated through the popularity of "Stitch and Bitch" groups internationally, this form of fiction positions knitting as integral to the narrative. Knitting contributes to the development and connection of characters, drives the narrative and is used as a description of place, space and time. As items are knitted stitch by stitch, time progresses minute by minute. Knit Lit encompasses two established genres, both aimed at a female readership: the murder mystery, and Chick Lit, or in these examples, Chick Knit Lit.

Here, I intend to discuss the ways in which Knit Lit represents the knitting woman to a contemporary audience, questioning whether this character has developed from more traditional and stereotypical incarnations arising from the iconology of femininity. The impetus therefore is to question the ways in which narrative construction and characterisation within Knit Lit can be understood as representative of contemporary femininity. By outlining the two generic strands of Knit Lit, considering the novels, and making comparisons with earlier examples of knitting women in fiction, I will assess the construction of modes of femininity and map the move of knitting from sub-text to narrative, questioning the role of knitting as a metaphor and barometer of female morality.

Knitting has always, to a certain extent, been gendered. In relation to employment or paid knitting, labour was sexually divided and/or spatially distanced from the world of work, thus limiting remuneration for workers. By the time knitting became a middle class leisure pursuit in the late eighteenth century it had been completely domesticated and thus associated with women; women's work, women's pastimes, and therefore the iconology of knitting was intrinsically linked to the construction and maintenance of a feminine ideal. From this perspective, knitting and femininity were inseparable, and therefore knitting could become a metaphor for women or a woman, as in Daphné du Maurier's *Rebecca*, or a means of instruction and demonstration of how women should act and behave.

To associate knitting with morality and the construction of a feminine ideal, is to suggest that knitting is a tool of patriarchy and as such can be employed to re-establish and maintain the status quo. Knitting, under these circumstances, instills codes and patterns of behaviour deemed socially suitable for women. For example, obedience and patience obtained as a result of learning and practicing knitting, diligence through the adherence to rules outlined in patterns, quietness whilst engaging in a specific and absorbing activity, usefulness of labour through the construction of garments, dish cloths, and so on. One might conclude that knitting is merely another activity which isolates women and encourages them to "suffer and be still".[2]

Reading, on the other hand, might be considered as a more subversive pastime. Although it requires quiet focus and contemplation, reading fiction in particular is a non-productive activity, there is no specific end product, and therefore such pursuits can be considered "wasteful" and "indulgent".[3] Similarly, reading fiction aimed at women compounds the concept of uselessness; texts encourage fantasy, emphasise romance, and promote a benign escapism.

Knitting in literature pays homage to such feminine attributes. But it does not merely reproduce them as a form of moral instruction, even when referred to or presented as norms of accepted behaviour and practice. For example, the invisibility, inquisitiveness and resourcefulness of women is demonstrated through the crime writing of Agatha Christie and Patricia Wentworth who portray knitting as an innocuous pastime undertaken by clever but nosy old ladies such as Misses Marple and Silver. Knitting in these texts acts as a guise, a means of concealment, which combined with the stereotype of the elderly spinster, creates an invisibility; a woman devoid of any display of sexuality. This invisibility facilitates keen and clever observation from the margins of the narrative mystery. Indeed, it is precisely the stereotyping applied to seemingly sexless women, and knitting, that enable both women to contribute so ably to solving the mystery without critiquing the type itself. Both characters rely on women's intuition rather than rationality, but nonetheless such a practice distinguishes the female from the male sleuth, assigning femininity to the biologically deterministic binaries of female/nature/irrationality, versus male/culture/rationality.

Similarly the amateur status of Marple and the lack of discussion regarding financial remuneration in the *Miss Silver Mysteries*, distance both of the characters from the world of paid employment and remove the opportunity for the articulation of power. They cannot make arrests or bring perpetrators to justice. For this they must rely on the cooperation of the exclusively male police force. Both characters, therefore, become a sign of the paradoxical potential of women and an expression of their powerlessness within a patriarchal framework. One might suggest that they are products of inter-war society; and like the vast majority of ordinary women of the period both are understood as valuable but not valued. In both examples the reader is encouraged to accept and positively acknowledge gender differences rather than challenging them, and once the mystery is solved, Marple and Silver return to their knitting.

In Knit Lit mysteries, the ghosts of Marple and Silver linger. Although the women in these contemporary texts are equally products of the times, they bear witness to a history of female, amateur or outsider detectives. Knitting is not merely an aspect of iconography, as with earlier mysteries, but a central theme running throughout each text. Indeed, descriptions of knitting a particular item or garment runs parallel with the narrative. As the story unfolds, the knitting grows, as would be the case in traditional textile stories which were performed orally.[4] The correlation between narrative and the making process exemplifies the passing of real time, whilst also enabling the articulation of gesture and hand-brain coordination. Knitting here is not solely a means of marking time and driving the narrative, it is presented as active, aggressive even, with texts featuring murder victims skewered to death with knitting needles and restrained or smothered with knitting yarn. Murder is often perpetrated by women, and crimes solved by them, and therefore the premise, protagonists and narrative are female dominated and motivated. Knitting in these texts is both pleasurable and horrific, exerting the potential to both heal and harm. As a result knitting extends beyond the hidden and unassuming as in earlier murder mysteries. Knitting women move from the margins to centre stage.

THE YARN SHOP

The focal site of each Knit Lit novel is a yarn shop and the narrative unfolds amidst this setting. Within these largely rural communities, knitting is often part of daily life, people keep sheep and alpaca, spin and dye their own yarns, and sell them to the yarn shop. Concepts of production and consumption are important elements within the setting. A firm emphasis on DIY and traditional methods of production, from animal rearing, hand-spinning, alongside knitting one's own clothing from one's own patterns, is juxtaposed with the opportunity for the purchase of kits, yarns and other knit related ephemera. Lavish descriptions of the shops' layout and stock entice the reader into a state of consumerist desire. In the yarn shop, the reader finds a mix of the traditional with the modern, an ideal world in which local businesses support local suppliers, and where traditional practices and products merge with the latest fashions and yarn technology.

In these communities, everyone knows everyone else, and the yarn shop, which is also the meeting point for knitting groups, becomes a place not merely for consumerism, but

also discussion, highlighting the contemporary impact of Stitch and Bitch groups whilst referring to the history of the knitting circle. In these instances, the yarn shop is significant for the formation of the narrative and characters. It offers a predominantly female space, which unlike the communal focal point of the pub, as in British soap opera, is concerned with specifically female interests and can be seen as respectable and seemingly non-threatening. In Maggie Sefton's *A Deadly Yarn*, we see the escapist potential of the yarn shop:

> Kelly concentrated on the deep rose circlet of yarn, stitches rhythmically adding row after row to the sweater-in-the-round. She'd been sitting at the shop's library table for over two hours this morning. Just like yesterday, she'd found herself unable to start on her usual morning routine at the computer. She'd work on client accounts later. Right now, Kelly wanted to be surrounded by the warmth of the shop, where she could talk to friends and people she'd grown to care about these last six months. She needed to be here.[5]

The yarn shop provides a locale in which contemporary women can meet and engage in traditionally female pastimes; a place where they can feel safe, and as such creates an environment which is both comforting and nostalgic. The warmth of the yarn, the repetition of the stitches, the cosiness of knitted items, combine with a sense of an all-embracing community working in harmony together. This is knitting as an ideal.

This idyllic setting is thrown into disarray when a murder occurs. In several books, the murder takes place in the yarn shop, which destroys the physical and metaphorical harmony of the environment. For example, in Monica Ferris's *Crewel World*, Betsy Devonshire, the book's protagonist and reluctant amateur sleuth, returns to the yarn shop:

> Betsy could not believe the disarray. The floor was covered with yarn and floss. The spin racks were on their sides, magazines had been crumpled and ripped, baskets that had held knitting yarn had not only been emptied, but stepped on…. Behind the chair was a big heap of wool and books, and beyond them, as if they had been moved aside to uncover her, was a woman.[6]

The implied anger Betsy feels at the disturbance of the shop, in particular that the wool had been "stepped on", suggests a moral outrage which seems more significant than the discovery of the body. The implication is that anyone who is so disrespectful of yarn, could equally be responsible for murder. In *Crewel World*, the discovery of the body—Betsy's sister, and the owner of the yarn shop—is an expression of chaos in a stable world. Here justice is to be sought, not merely as a means of retribution, but as a means of restoring harmony to the whole community.

For Betsy Devonshire, the discovery of a body in the yarn shop may well be the catalyst for the restoration of loss to what was once an 'ideal'. But in other novels, knitting is a site of aggression, and therefore the threat comes from within. For example, in Mary Kruger's *Died in the Wool*, Ariadne

Evans, proprietor of 'Ariadne's Web', finds a client dead in the shop: "'ohmygod', she gasped. A purple wool homespun yarn was tangled about Edith's neck and tied back to two sticks into a crude, but effective garrotte."[7]

Not only is the calm sanctuary of the shop disturbed, but the victim is a knitter, and the killer has a clear knowledge of yarn which is intended to apportion blame to another—the maker of the homespun yarn. Here knitting is both active and pro-active, utilised as a means of death and motivator for its punishment, exercising the potential for the hobby to both harm and heal, to destroy and restore. Knitting becomes the site, weapon, and thematic link between the key players in the narrative, and is therefore instrumental in unlocking or unravelling the mystery.

KNITTING DETECTIVES

Once the murder has been committed, the knitting group is mobilised, with each member exhibiting a skill or area of expertise, which helps decipher a clue. This is more than a reliance on 'women's intuition'. The women in contemporary mysteries are amateur experts. In Mary Kruger's *Knit Fast; Die Young*, for example, Ariadne Evans is able to identify a yarn with forensic accuracy.[8] This implies that women have useful and rational skills, albeit obtained through the knowledge of a traditional female pastime, which perform a vital role in solving a murder. Women are presented as having distinct individual skills, rather than accessing a homogeneous series of traits. They are also presented as flawed, making mistakes and feeling fear, whilst also displaying a sense of fun and humour. This is evidenced in the language of the texts, which frequently utilise puns:

> While Josh pieces together the details of the crime, clues about Ariadne's ties to Miss Perry come to light… and a bizarre pattern unfolds. Now it's up to Ariadne to do some sleuthing of her own. Can she untangle the investigation without getting snarled up into too much trouble? That depends on whether the killer is as crafty as she is….[9]

The humorous use of rather corny puns might imply that these mysteries are fun or light-hearted, rather than exhibiting gritty realism that is the preserve of the male detective. Although crimes are often gratuitous—stabbing with knitting needles, smothering with fleeces, falling from high railings—their description is limited, leaving the details to the imagination of the reader, implying a sense of propriety and decency, which sanitises and feminises murder. The emphasis on the female 'detective' as an amateur also reflects a desire to 'clean up' crime, offering a rather domestic and nostalgic return to the women in murder mysteries of the past, rather than emulating contemporary and popular professional women investigators such as Kay Scarpetta in Patricia Cornwell's novels.[10]

In each novel, the central character displays traits pertinent to a stereotype of a 'modern' woman. They are constructed to demonstrate business acumen, not usually associated with either women or knitters, but also display emotional independence. Whereas knitting women have previously been constructed as sexless spinsters, the women in these novels have all, at some stage, conformed to the societal and heterosexual norms of marriage. All are now divorced. This might suggest that these norms have been rejected, and the social order is under review. However, this is problematic, and although these women appear strong and independent, existing in situations which are on the whole female dominated, the insistence of a heterosexual past implies a particular norm, in which no space is created for homosexual women, yet the potential for heterosexual romance remains ever present. Although not a central element of the narrative, romance is certainly an aspect of the novels which is deemed to speak to a female readership, reflecting what might be described as "life narratives", whilst working structurally as a device to tie up loose ends creating a sense of 'wholeness' to the scenario. It appears that a single woman, however successful and independent, is still an awkward and out of place entity, which can only be completed or resolved by her possible joining to a man.[11]

MEN AND ROMANCE

In the knitting murder mysteries, the possibility for romance is never completely fulfilled. In each novel, romantic interest is presented in the form of a rather benign 'good man', often a policeman involved in solving the crime. Love is chaste, there is no sex, and the seeming impotency of the male romantic persona, re-establishes the potential empowerment of the female protagonist. Yet she is neither femme fatale nor slut and becomes the embodiment of a 'good woman', hardworking, honest, and largely without desire.[12] Lack of desire therefore can be assessed as a means of either transcending female stereotypes, which emphasise a reliance on overt sexuality to achieve their aims, or, as a means of promoting traditional values that oppose promiscuity. Either way, the absence of sex in these novels creates an unreality, reminiscent of a retrogressive gaze into a nostalgic world.

The female protagonists may appear to embrace traditional feminine virtues such as abstinence and nurturing and occupy their time with similarly traditional activities like knitting and baking, but they also display a fearlessness and tenacity which often endangers their lives. As each protagonist comes closer to unveiling the mystery, their lives become increasingly threatened, frequently coming to blows with the perpetrator. As the drama reaches its climax, women adopt the traditional male attributes of dominance and competition in the fight for justice, but once the villain is caught, the status quo is restored, and the hard-hitting women go back to their knitting.

Although these new knitting mysteries include youthful protagonists, they are ostensibly rural and steeped in a nostalgia, which assumes an older reader. Conversely, Chick Knit Lit emerges from an urban setting, includes 'fashionable' characters and by association, presumes a younger audience. Largely derivative of the romance, emphasising the importance of female friendships as well as finding a man, hungry for glamour and independence, juggling the pressures of a successful career, whilst dealing with life's ups and downs, Chick Lit offers a scenario deemed familiar to the contemporary woman.[13] Humour is at the forefront of these novels, which assumes that the genre is light-hearted and by association, light-reading, offering a fantasy or escapist arena for the discussion of everyday life. Such an assumption presupposes that writing for, about and by women, is itself less serious than other forms of writing, an approach highly contested by authors and readers alike.[14] Regardless of the seriousness of the genre, it has been extended to include a variety of hobbies and interests deemed suitable for a female readership. Therefore, Chick Knit Lit throws knitting into the mix, as a character in its own right, acting as a catalyst for change, personal development, meeting ground, means of independence or self-sufficiency.

Men in these texts are considered 'The Other', thus reversing rather than questioning the patriarchal 'Othering' of women. One might see this as a step towards equality albeit rather tenuous, or as a return to biological determinism, evidenced in contemporary popular sexual psychology and texts driven by the prospect of finding a partner.[15] The women in knitting novels appear to represent a generation of women who find Feminism outdated and its ideals at odds with a social and personal desire to settle down. Post-feminism enables women to find some equilibrium, the opportunity to 'have it all', satisfying a concept of gender equality whilst acknowledging gender difference. Women choose to knit for themselves, rather than for others, distancing themselves from the domestic associations of the craft. Here, knitting is more frivolous, expensive and glamorous. It is an expression of ones own creativity, achievement and personality. In, for example, *Knitting under the Influence*, when Lucy starts to make a sweater for her boyfriend, she is met with horror from her friends:

> 'You should only ever knit for yourself' Kathleen said. 'That's the first rule of the single girl's knitting handbook. It's the only rule.' She put down her work and held up her hand. 'You try to knit a guy a sweater, then one of two things will happen'—she raised her index finger—'either he'll break up with you just as you're finishing it, which means you have to destroy all your work or spend the rest of your life trying to find another guy exactly the same size, or'—another finger went up—'even if you do get to give it to him, he won't like it or even wear it and it'll make you so mad, you'll end up breaking up with him. And some future girlfriend of his will find it someday and tear it to pieces. Trust me, you only want to knit stuff for yourself.'[16]

FRIENDS

The support offered by the all-women fictional group gives the reader access to an 'ideal' set of 'friends' reminiscent of traditional, and seemingly lost, kinship networks. Each character is presented as a potential role model, active and successful achievers, people who engage in life rather than passively watch the world go by, whilst aping the roles and concerns of the reader. In *Diva's Don't Knit*, the distance between a lived life and the escapist or traditional pleasure of knitting is acknowledged:

> 'I'm really enjoying it. It's so nice in the evenings when I'm watching telly. It makes me feel like a proper mum, sitting there knitting. And it stops me eating crisps too' … 'I like it because it helps to pass the time while you're waiting for something exciting to happen' … 'you'll end up with a very long scarf if you're waiting for something to happen around here.'[17]

The praxis at which traditional female roles merge with the new, as outlined in the above quotation, highlights a contemporary dilemma faced by young women of achieving personal and societal goals, while actively participating in and determining their own lives. Essentially this can be understood as making the mundane extraordinary and it is from this perspective that knitting becomes a metaphor for life; something that takes a great deal of skill to master, requires effort and dedication to achieve perfection, but is also something that can be remedied or reconsidered by unpicking and re-doing. Goldsmith describes the perfection her character seeks:

> She liked perfection, but it seemed achievable only in very small things. When she looked at her life and the lives of others she saw nothing but disappointment, compromise, dropped stitches and twisted yarn…. Of course it was only a scarf, but she had made it with her own hands, her own vision and her own intelligence. Perhaps the secret to a perfect life, or something close to it, was to keep it small and pay attention.[18]

While feminists debate the recent revival of knitting as a pastime and as a sign of a return to patriarchal values, novels that feature knitting as a theme do little to counter-balance the argument.[19] The fictitious heroines of these novels may display characteristics of independence, but largely they are seduced by the possibility of romantic liaisons, traditional female relationships and the lure of consumer goods.

One might assume that the women in these texts are merely dressed up fragments of a variety of gender stereotypes. They embrace traditional domesticity and a quest for romantic love, yet acknowledge the significance of feminism in relation to their professional aspirations and personal attitudes. But the male characters are presented as equally paradoxical. Unlike Laura Mulvey's assertion that "men act and women appear" the converse is true in these texts, with male characters constructed as both potential hero and eunuch.[20] In these scenarios men have the potential to act, but when this happens it is through social constructs such as professional obligation rather than personal freedom. Therefore they are impotent, merely vague, two-dimensional characters who appear in the plot rather than moving it on. This is disconcerting. An impotent love interest reinforces concepts of the 'good' woman, denying female characters access to or negotiation of positions outside of the virgin/whore dichotomy.

CONCLUSION

The revival in knitting as a hobby has opened a market for subject specific writing for women, and as a consequence of the significance of the heritage product as a indicator of nostalgic yearning, novels which address the values of the past have become increasingly popular. Similarly, the popularity of Chick Lit and the new fashionability of knitting have created a market for young women, in which they are offered the opportunity to buy kits, instructions of how to knit a jumper in a day, and access to both cheap and very expensive yarn, enabling the highly portable pastime of knitting to fit into busy schedules, suit any budget, and satisfy fashion trends. Therefore, these books, like so many other aspects of women's lives, address women as consumers, not only through the purchase of the books themselves, but through their language and rhetoric, and the ways in which they romanticise accumulation.[21]

Contemporary Knit Lit embodies the traditional concept of knitting as a feminine activity, although not necessarily a domestic one. It celebrates the notion of female friendships, which could be argued are representative of a 'sisterhood', challenging notions of knitting, and indeed, reading, as passive and patriarchal pastimes. For characters, knitting becomes not just a means of forging and maintaining dynamic female groupings, but is also as a metaphor for life narratives, which unravel and are re-knitted as part of the story. In addition, knitting becomes a motivator and skill set which enables women to not only take care of themselves, but also solve crime and address personal crisis in a pragmatic manner. Similarly, these texts offer the reader a form of escapism not dissimilar to other genres of fiction aimed at women, such as romance. However, knitting fiction offers more than wishful thinking. It offers escape through practical engagement, not merely with the narrative, but with the patterns additional to, but featured in, the texts. This suggests that the seemingly passive act of reading now offers the potential for interaction and activity.

The stories told bear witness to genres historically aimed at women, offering well worn formulas that reinstate rather than challenge the dominance of patriarchy. One might conclude that whilst traditional stories are revived alongside traditional crafts practices, we are witness to a revitalisation of activities presumed lost as a result of both industrialisation and Modernism, and from a feminist perspective, this can be viewed as a means of uncovering hidden histories, previously deemed part of an inherently feminine folk culture.[22] Indeed, in each example of Knit Lit discussed, both women's creative practice and their ability to make something from nothing, becomes synonymous with women's struggles with daily life. Making both makes meaning for the women as well as providing the means through which their problems are communicated, worked through and overcome. Knitting becomes both a metaphor for daily life, but also a tool for making space, making special and for making friends and communities, activities and ideals otherwise hidden, forgotten or lost.

As women return to pick up their needles, and cast on once more, the history of women's relationships to knitting and narratives becomes woven into the fabric of contemporary femininity. Knitting offers women a connection with the past, engagement in a practice undertaken by women through time, as well as a means of expressing creativity, of making something from nothing, forming inter-personal relationships and accessing the latest trends. This can be seen as a merging of the new with the old, a means of situating women and women's creative practice within a framework which has stability in a world with none. The problem, it seems, is that contemporary representations of women who knit may merely be, like the literary genres, rather formulaic, repetitive in both practice and ideology, offering a re-worked escapism rather than a solution to patriarchy.

An earlier version of this text appears in *The Culture of Knitting*, reprinted here with kind permission of Berg Publishers, an imprint of A&C Black Publishers Ltd.

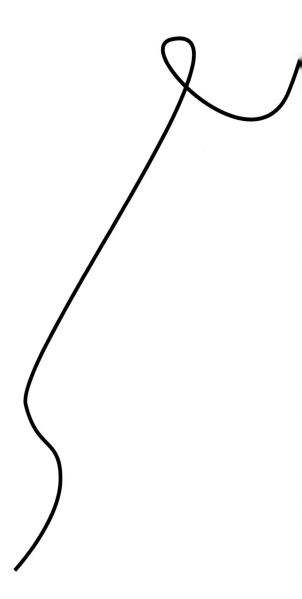

ALTER EGOS

MARK NEWPORT

Batman, Iron Man, Spiderman and the Rawhide Kid—these characters are childhood memories of the ultimate man—the Dad every boy wants, the man every boy wants to grow up to be. My hand knit acrylic re-creations of these heroes' costumes combine their heroic, protective, ultra masculine, yet vulnerable, personas with the protective gestures of my mother—hand knit acrylic sweaters meant to keep me safe from New England winters. The costumes are life-size, my size, wearable objects that hang limply on hangers challenging the standard muscular form of the hero and offering the space for someone to imagine themselves wearing the costume, becoming the hero. They become the uniforms I can wear to protect my family from the threats—bullies, murderers, terrorists, paedophiles, and fanatical messianic characters —we are told surround us.

The *Flamer*, *Naftaman*, *W-man*, and *Every-Any-No Man* are heroes of my own invention. They push the image of the hero by highlighting knitting materials, textures, and traditions —cables and the use of "ends" to make a sweater—in the form of the costume. Some of the colour and texture choices are based on the sweaters my mother made, her love of cables and her colour choices. In these I work to forge the link between childhood experience and an adult understanding of protection, masculinity, and heroism.

Performances, prints, and photographs are my opportunity to expand the narratives the suits suggest to me. While earlier works in print and photography focused on the hero in the costume, where and how he functions, these pieces start to explore the alter ego within the costume and the connotations of knitting in relation to various roles and activities. Knitting remains the questionable activity for the protagonist while costumes change to more socially accepted garb. In each scenario the knitting seems out of place or defensive. How do these different stereotypes of men relate to an activity like knitting?

MARK NEWPORT, *Flamer*, 2008. Hand knit acrylic and buttons,
203 x 58.5 x 15 cm.

right MARK NEWPORT, *Every-Any-No-Man*, 2005. Hand knit acrylic and buttons, 305 x 63.5 x 15 cm.
opposite left MARK NEWPORT, *W-man*, 2009. Hand knit acrylic and buttons, 203 x 58.5 x 15 cm.
opposite right MARK NEWPORT, *Naftaman*, 2008. Hand knit acrylic and buttons, 203 x 58.5 x 15 cm.

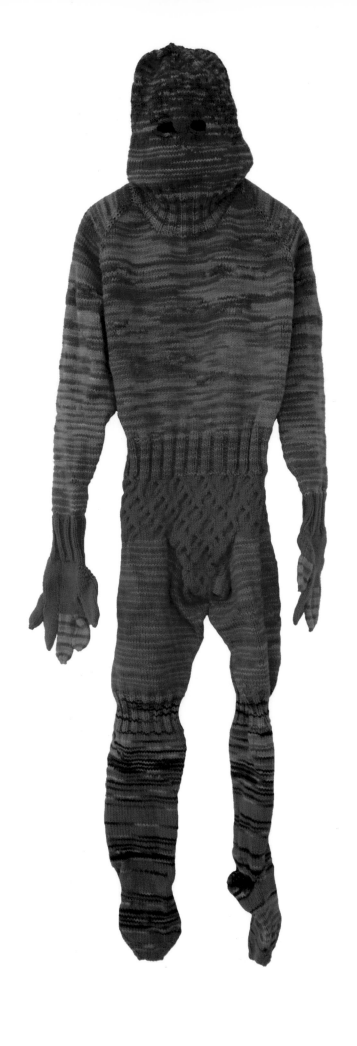

MARK NEWPORT, *Alter Egos: Zack Reads*, 2009.
Archival ink jet print, 33 x 48 cm.

MARK NEWPORT, *Alter Egos: Backstage*, 2009.
Archival ink jet print, 33 x 48 cm.

above MARK NEWPORT, *Alter Egos: Practice*, 2009.
Archival ink jet print, 48 x 33 cm.
opposite MARK NEWPORT, *Alter Egos: Cowboy*, 2009.
Archival ink jet print, 48 x 33 cm.

FINDING YOUR WAY HOME

JEANETTE SENDLER

Moder Dy or 'mother-wave' is the name for a series of strong outgoing waves spreading out from the Shetland Isles caused by deep, incoming ocean currents. For centuries before widespread use of the compass, fishermen in open boats were aware of the *Moder Dy*, and used its 'sight' and 'sound' to navigate their homeward journeys.

> I've heard of fisherman winning home
> that way; but running before a storm
> you'd need ear eyes
> to sound a home wave,
> see a mother in water
> —Robin Munro

At home, the fishermen's wives estimated when their husbands would return by the amount of yarn knitted in their absence. *Finding Your Way Home* reconnects with this natural way of time-keeping, in stark contrast to the speed of twenty-first century life.

Large-scale knitted installations made from Shetland wool, echo these traditions, and are informed by my evolving relationship with the island and its rich and inspiring traditions. The work speaks of the *Moder Dy* and its navigational role, as well as the innate, internal rhythms employed by the women to measure their men folk's return.

previous pages JEANETTE SENDLER, *Finding Your Way Home*, 2006.
Shetland wool, machine knitted. Photograph by fordfokus.

KNITTING IN SOUTHERN AFRICAN FICTION

JESSICA HEMMINGS

Betty LaDuke, in her study of visual art in Zimbabwe, writes:

> The missionary legacy in Zimbabwe is two-fold. In addition to the cross, the other visible but seldom discussed tool is the crochet hook. This tool has become a subtle means of encouraging women's passive creativity as they produced endless yards of intricately designed white tablecloths and doilies for upper-class White and Black Africans and tourists.[1]

LaDuke's "passive creativity" contributed to the once vibrant tourist economy of the region. Its new place in the fiction of southern Africa is quite different.

For practical purposes, I have conflated knitting and crochet in this section. Admittedly, the two methods of textile production are not identical, but share the common method of construction from a single thread. More importantly, both are foreign imports to the landscapes and cultures I will discuss. While the current popularity of knitting can be charted by its presence in much contemporary fiction, the roles it adopts in the southern African context are often unexpected. Floss M Jay's short story "Knitting Gloves", 1983, tackles the seemingly incompatible issues of maternal obligation and sexual fantasy. Brian Chikwava's unreliable narrator deploys knitting to construct an image of the narrator's late mother in *Harare North*, 2009. Finally Tsitsi Dangarembga uses knitting to illustrate racially defined loyalties in pre-independence Zimbabwe in her most recent novel *The Book of Not*, 2006. In all three cases knitting is written as an object and action far more complex in associations and meanings than the "passive creativity" previously assigned to the craft.

"KNITTING GLOVES" BY FLOSS M JAY

In the four brief pages of text South African author Floss M Jay uses to write "Knitting Gloves", we are shown how the presence of knitting can work to both confirm assumptions of domestic life and violently disrupt any comfortable sense of familiarity. The single perspective of the narrative is told from the point of view of the main character, Meg, providing the reader with few concrete clues to judge fantasy from reality. What is clear is that knitting exists in the real world, a fact that provides a comforting counterpoint to the short story's often-unexpected content.

First introduced sitting "on a long green couch" we meet Meg "knitting another glove, a striped one, the kind which has each finger a different colour".[2] Almost immediately there is a suggestion of doubt, if not for the time we can imagine Meg is investing in this production, then in the design of the outcome. The glove pattern comes from a French pattern book suggesting that Meg is following something relatively complex, sealed with the approval of a publication. But despite the skill required to knit the multicoloured gloves, they are thought by her unnamed husband to be "silly" in contrast to the "plain, navy blue gloves" he prefers.[3] In this small trivial detail, a picture of a passionless marriage appears. An activity Meg enjoys is dismissed by her husband, a character of such unimportance that the narrator does not even assign him a name.

Others benefit from Meg's knitting. "Friends all over the country" receive her knitted gloves in varying sizes according to their identity in life as child, woman or man.[4] The existence of recipients for Meg's efforts, shows her to be less isolated than her solitary craft first suggests. As well as occupying time, her production links her to a community otherwise absent from the narrative. Curiously, this opening scene concludes with the narrator admitting that "Meg also thought them [the coloured gloves] silly, but she preferred them."[5] A tension is established between Meg's awareness and sympathy for her husband's conservative taste and the frivolity of multicoloured fingers that she finds preferable to the other mundane options life has in store.

With the exception of knitting, all other details refereed to in the story are bleak. A winter garden with "only stalks and dry leaves, and the drizzle blank" faces Meg whose "loose fat give[s] way under the pressure" of her arms crossing her stomach.[6] Dull discontent is brewing, both in the setting she inhabits and the body she occupies. But these descriptions of knitting, followed by domestic details lull us into a false, if depressing, sense of security. This familiarity is punctuated abruptly by dialogue from an unfamiliar character: "I want to fuck hard," David said, "smiling in her ear.[7] We know Meg to be the recipient of this comment because she "is sweating, her hair stringy, her back wet against the brown sheet of an unfamiliar mattress."[8] But it remains unconfirmed if David is the same man who prefers the safety of navy blue gloves to his wife's multicoloured creations. Somehow it seems unlikely that a man, whose choice of knitted gloves is so conservative, is the voice behind such sexually explicit dialogue.

Time skips again and before the first page of this brief short story has concluded, the reader is shown three snapshots in no particular chronological order. Gloves are knit. David speaks. Then Meg recalls "white flowers in her garden in springtime", a moment presumably at least nine months removed from the winter scene Meg now observes while knitting.[9] Few chronological clues are provided, other than the observation that the spring garden scene with its filigree white flowers "puffing into the air all over the garden" "was in the spring, before David, and summer".[10] David, it seems, is not a man in need of knitted winter gloves. By the end of the first page we have returned to the "grey stone of the garden walls [that] was almost black from rain" and "nappies on the line".[11] David, real or imagined, is absent and somewhere in this cramped world of Meg's coloured gloves, overweight tummy and sexual fantasies is a child.

Steps count out the cramped proportions of the narrative's setting. "Four paces away, was the wall with the sash window."[12] With heavy thighs, the "weight of [which] made it impossible for her to move fast" Meg walks the "Three steps in the passage up to the child's room."[13] The surprises the narrative has provided until this point can be made more comfortable if explained as dream or fantasy. But Meg's observations of her sleeping child are harder to dismiss as memory or fantasy. The broken capillaries on her child's temples disgust her. Observing the "burgeoning child" she wills it to "shut up and don't live" before entering another fantasy, this time of castration.[14] It is unclear if the castrated male is her husband or her lover, but her husband becomes the likely candidate when the narrator reveals, "The child will never know that it is you who pretend to father her. I've made a fact of this emptiness."[15]

After drawing the reader through these disconcerting details, Meg leaves her sleeping child unharmed saying, "See you later. I'm going to knit some more."[16] Knitting signals a return to the reality of daily matter, the concrete and tangible that resides in stark contrast to her fantasies of violence and sexual pleasure. Gorging herself in the kitchen, a landscape of mindless repetitions appears. It is a place where Meg "could not separate this bread from the bread of nine o'clock" consumed just an hour earlier.[17] The garden she looks out on and the food she eats are written as: "all the same. All grey. Like the garden. And tasted of nothing."[18] Knitting provides the only source of colour.

When the television is finally flicked on, Meg "picked up her knitting, found the place, and began to knit."[19] The "wool a deep, rust colour, the colour of the deepest recesses of her womb" suggests the menstrual blood that would have been absent during her pregnancy.[20] Meg knits, as though her knitting has some intimate relationship to the creation of a child her body has made. "She made a finger while the television showed her more pictures."[21] Her actions create another object that is both functional and hopefully joyous, antithetical feelings to those she has for her child and husband/lover.

The introduction of the television's external narrative in the closing sentences of the short story provides us with another potential source of escape. Can the abrupt interjections of violence and sexual fantasy be explained as the intrusion of the world of television, invading the domestic quiet of her home and knitting? The suggestion is easier than confronting the message that Meg is mother to an unwanted child, married to a hated husband, knitting to while away hours in her domestic trap, while dreaming of sex and castration.

Without the comfortable and relatable pastime of knitting, Meg may become too extreme a character for the reader. Her knitting provides a hook that signals she is not entirely foreign, but a woman engaged with actions that are familiar and benign.

Knitting allows us to push the shocking revelations of her other world out of reality and comfortably assign to them other explanations (dream sequence, television input). Meg's knitting may take on LaDuke's description of "passive creativity", but it stands disconcertingly close to thoughts and actions that are far from passive. Without the solid and relatable presence of knitting this bizarre narrative would become easy to dismiss.

BRIAN CHIKWAVA'S
HARARE NORTH

Brian Chikwava uses a similar technique of unreliability in *Harare North*, a novel set in London. Here, again, we are reliant on the perspective of a single unnamed male narrator. Without the voices of other characters to confirm or deny the narrator's story, the reader is left in the similar position to "Knitting Gloves", wondering what is real and imagined within the world of the story. From the novel's first page, Chikwava's narrator sets himself apart by his use of a distinctive speech pattern. Laden with irony, the unfamiliar syntax and grammar he adopts provides the reader with the ongoing possibility for misreading.

When Chikwava's narrator finally arrives, after detention at Heathrow Airport, at a friend's house in East London, he brings with him "a small bag of groundnuts from Zimbabwe; groundnuts that my aunt bring from she rural home".[22] The well-meaning gift is rejected without thought by Sekai, his friend's wife, who "give the bag one look and bin it right in front of me. She say I should never have been allow to bring them nuts into the country because maybe they carry disease. Then she go out and buy us McDonald's supper."[23]

City living replaces rural values in one fell swoop, but the irony of it is clear to the narrator. Along with his traditional gift, our narrator also brings with him some of his own traditional values. Observing disharmony in his friend's marriage, he notes that "Things will have been better if he had do something about Sekai, like maybe giving she some small baby to keep she busy. But this have not happen since they get married and Sekai know how to play Paul now."[24] A feminist this protagonist is not. But the role of humour and the unfailing unreliability of the narrator's observations conspire to draw the reader into a world where fact and fiction are impossible to separate.

The night of the narrator's twenty-second birthday he "go to bed early" thinking that Paul and Sekai's unwelcoming home is "wrong place to celebrate birthday." In the three italicised pages of text that follow, we are introduced to his late mother. Again, the timing of the passage just before bedtime, and its disconnection from dialogue attributed to any other characters suggests a dream sequence. "*Since she funeral*," we learn, "*she have knit herself back into life.*"[25] This ambiguous statement leaves all the information to follow open to interpretation. The passage could be a memory or a dream. But "knit" could also refer not to textiles, but the ways in which the memory of his mother has kept her connected to his waking life. Furthermore, the unfamiliar syntax and grammar Chikwava uses throughout the novel

makes it easy to dismiss the sentence as a misreading or misunderstanding on the part of the reader. Perhaps it is since someone else's funeral that the mother has worked to reconnect with friends and family? This strategy works to place constant doubt on the part of the reader, who must work to decipher the narrator's story as though reading in an unfamiliar language, which is precisely the narrator's experience in his new British homeland.

Chikwava writes: "*She expect friends. The kettle on the stove begin to shake lid, letting steam out. Mother throw easy look at it and continue sweeping. Your house is like your head, she say to sheself, you have to keep sweeping it clean if you want to stay sane.*"[26] The suggestion of insanity further disrupts our trust of the information we are receiving. Has his mother suffered from mental problems? Has our narrator witnessed or even inherited tendencies that would further complicate his telling of a truthful recollection of events? Considering the fact that he has only recently arrived in London, it is curious that his mother is already unconcerned at the cost of the bicycle repair she is facing, "*because she have son in Harare North who can pay for all this*".[27] Here too time can make unreal leaps.

In preparation for the arrival of guests, mother starts to "*dust up inside house… Mother's bestest tea set, and water-glass sets. They is one them white doilies which she have knit all her life. On them glasses is the hens that she knit when she find she have nothing to do.*"[28] Much like "Knitting Gloves" craft is described as a way to pass time, here adopting a decorative function alongside the purchased ornaments. We know that the narrator's mother has had her funeral, nonetheless, "*There is half-finished red hen; soon it will be finished and stuffed with cotton wool and put inside display cabinet.*"[29] This slippage reveals time to be nonlinear. There is knitting yet to be completed and a time in the dead woman's near future when this can take place.

While knitting occupies her idle time it provides a social function shared by a community of friends with which mother shares patterns and teaches:

> *Mother show she friends how to knit them hens over pot of Tanganda Tea. They scribble down them details; wool colour code and all. She dig out the rest of them photos of me in Harare North—me I am feeding them pigeons in this big city. Mother go into show-off style, telling friends yea he is my son that one. Them other women look them photographs; they tea go cold.*[30]

Before the passages in italics come to an end the narrator describes how "*I settle over she like Mist, mother… I suck thumb and nod. Mother hold me to she bosom and rock me gentle.*"[31] This tactic adds to the shock of the passage that follows, written in another voice: "Mother, she die of overdose. They carry she to hospital in wheelbarrow and she don't come back."[32] How do we reconcile the image of a woman sharing knitted hen patterns with her friends and the image of a woman taken to hospital in a wheelbarrow, dead from an overdose? Much like the conflicting thoughts shared by the narrator of "Knitting Gloves", knitting is used to lull the reader into a sense of familiarity by establishing a domestic environment which is not difficult to imagine, before introducing 'facts' that challenge our expectations of the character. As our narrator becomes increasingly unreliable, these early details and their reference to knitting are thrown into an even harsher light. The knitting described in the italicised passage may represent one facet of an entirely imagined identity the narrator has created for an imagined mother. By the conclusion of *Harare North*, the reader learns that it is impossible to know fact from fiction in the world Chikwava makes for us.

TSITSI DANGAREMBGA'S *THE BOOK OF NOT*

A final example of knitting in recent fiction from southern Africa occupies the more temporary domestic setting of the boarding school. Dangarembga's *The Book of Not*, introduces the sharp racial divisions at work in a European-style boarding school, The Young Ladies College of the Sacred Heart, in what was the British colony of Southern Rhodesia. Here our protagonist, Tambudzai Sigauke or Tambu, is one of a small group of black students, taken in by the Christian boarding school as token gestures of charity. Academically talented, Tambu pushes herself to achieve in a peculiar combination of arrogance and naive desire, both for herself and the praise of her uncle, Babamukuru, who finances her education.

The narrative begins with another example of shocking imagery. This time we read of a limb: "Up, up, up, the leg spun. A piece of a person, up there in the sky."[33] The leg belongs to the narrator's sister, Netsai, who has been helping the freedom fighters in the guerilla war against the white Rhodesian military. But after this initial introduction to her sister's experience, Tambu seems to immerse herself in her studies and a desire for self-improvement, blocking the incident from her consciousness. The strategy is one of survival: "If you went to school with white people and sat next to them in class, wouldn't you end up telling them something? One day the white people would discover my sister's activities."[34]

Knitting appears in the second half of the novel, when the white twin sisters, the Swanepoels, are orphaned. Their parents' murder is described by the newspaper image handed out amongst the students:

There was a quarter page sized photograph of a man sprawled out on the soil of his farm as though worshipping some old earth goddess. He had an axe in his head, carving the cranium into two equal half moons, so that it looked as though his head, perhaps because of his thoughts, has curiously turned into his buttocks. The man was Mr Swanepoel.[35]

After denouncing the violence, the sisters of the school invite those who are interested "to join women knitting comforters and gloves for the troops".[36] Tambu's decision to join the white women's knitting group is described with imagery reminiscent of the language used to describe her sister's horrific injury:

The impossibility of it, of the putting up of four fingers, of the stretching up of a hand on an arm, and then the impossibility of everything else after that moment of raising up, impossible because legs and other limbs you knew of tangled in heaps as they fell, tramped through my thoughts like a too heavy armed force.[37]

The girls of Tambu's own dormitory observe her knitting efforts with contempt, "Aren't there other people she sits with now?... these new people of hers, the ones where she goes knitting!"[38] Here knitting is not set in contrast to other shocking elements of the narrative. Instead it is directly implicated in the war effort. Knitting denotes loyalty to a cause, and in this case the cause is that of the white Rhodesian soldiers. One of Tambu's roommates questions her:

What if vana sisi who clean this room see this kind of thing in this room in this cupboard? She waved my ball of wool and knitting needles at me as though they were monstrous weapons direct from a brutal dictator's arsenal.... Which one of us will still be speaking if the elder siblings decide some people here must stop being sell-outs![39]

Vana sisi, a cleaner, will be a black woman subject to the same possibility of violence that threatens all the black students' families. Tambu's knitting takes on the burden of meaning far greater than the overturning of domestic expectations or passivity seen in the previous two examples. Here knitting comes to represent taking sides in a war for independence.

Inter-spliced with this violence is Tambu's almost impossible innocence. Trying to justify her knitting, she explains to her black roommates, "When the Swanepoels come back, I thought if... maybe someone said, I knitted a helmet and some gloves, I thought maybe it would help them, I finished quietly."[40] A father who "had an axe in his head, carving the cranium into two equal half moons", we know, will not need a helmet.[41] Nor will knitting mend the amputated limb her sister now endures. Dangarembga borrows the popular and relatable image of knitting, but infuses it with the violence and segregation of her narrative's setting. In doing so she provides yet another example of southern African literature, adopting a pastime that enjoys currency today, but expands on the power play LaDuke observes to be at work in this "passive creativity".

In the three examples of southern African fiction discussed, knitting grounds narratives that contain challenging and unexpected details. Jay depicts knitting as a passive and solitary activity. But its presence frames information that is far from passive, heightening the shock value and contrasting the experience of the lived and the imagined. Chikwava draws upon the craft to construct a positive image of the narrator's mother, before then revealing information in direct conflict with the domestic stability knitting has helped to conjure. Dangarembga uses knitting to reveal the conflicting loyalties her main character faces in pre-independence Zimbabwe. Here knitting is about power, noted by LaDuke, that is defined by wealth and race. In manipulating the assumptions we as readers bring to the craft, each author offers an image of the craft that is entirely dynamic, rather than passive, in its creativity.

SITE &
ACTIVIST KN

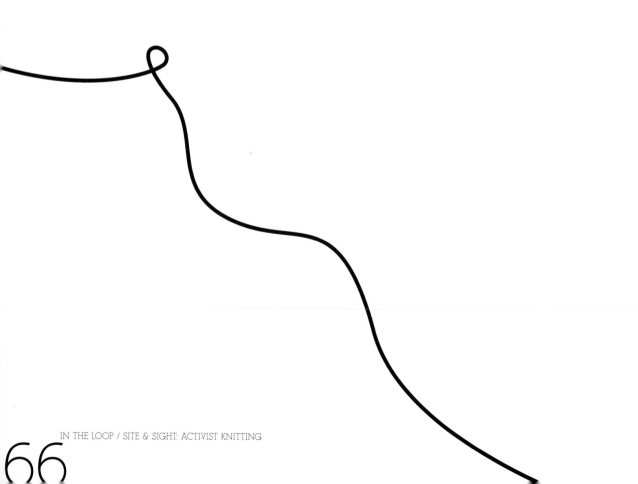

SIGHT:
TTING

Knitting and activism are two actions that do not initially seem to have much in common. Curiously, it may be precisely this misfit that makes knitting a popular tool for social protest today. Scale is a defining factor of the work in this section. Perhaps because knitting is so often created to the size of our bodies, its appearance on a large-scale is both unsettling and provocative.

Kirsty Robertson begins this section with her discussion of activism in the classroom. Acknowledging that "politics in the classroom is a precarious business", Robertson admits to "banking strongly on the perception of textiles as ultimately non-threatening and familiar" as a way to begin fostering critical thinking in her students. Her inspiring account of the textile's potential within education confronts the gaps in practical knowledge and critical thinking that can be endemic in affluent classroom settings around the world.

Deirdre Nelson shares her own version of 'quiet' activism, this time generated from her artistic practice. In recent years Nelson has taken on a number of projects, which engage not only with local communities, but also include a fundraising component. Unlike Robertson who tells of students largely separated from craft skills, Nelson's projects move into communities where residents were able to knit, or were cajoled and persuaded to try. The tangible outcomes have allowed both experts and novices to harness knitting for its fundraising potential.

Liz Collins' *Knitting Nation* moves machine knitting outside the individual's studio and into the realm of collaborative practice and performance art. Collins mobilises teams of machine knitters who knit on a massive scale, taking up specific agendas with each incarnation of the event. The cloth created by *Knitting Nation* has found itself draped from buildings, across parks and paraded through city streets; tackling issues as varied as the iconography of the gay pride flag and sweat shop labour.

Sophie Horton's experience with large-scale installations suggests a curious sense of threat which knitting, when large and public, seems to present. Like Collins, Horton has created massive knitted installations and muses in her contribution as to why fuzzy thread can raise such alarm and even hostility.

Lycia Trouton discusses two recent global movements that share an interest in "the body, touch and a search for love without fear": Internet Sex Blogging and Craftivism. Using the work of Rozzi George as an example, she finds shared motivations between the "playful and poverty-stricken" medium of knitting and the frank sex-memoire.

Finally, Lacey Jane Roberts shares her strategies of 'queering' her 'craft' practice, and explains her desire to work with knitting precisely because it provides the opportunity to overturn comfortable stereotypes. She explains her use of knitting as a desire to "break down the classifications of art, craft, design and architecture in an attempt to thwart the categorization of my practice".

If we accept that we no longer need to knit to keep warm, then what the contributors in this section offer are inspiring examples of how knitting has adopted other vital functions within contemporary communities. Inevitably, the new positions each seeks to negotiate for their work is under constant threat of appropriation. But I suspect that these artists, activists and educators will remain one step ahead of the category makers that seek to lay claim to their work.

TEXTILES AND ACTIVISM

KIRSTY ROBERTSON

As artists and academics we tend to talk and write quite a bit about our research and our practices. In my experience, we tend to talk much less often about teaching, although it arguably occupies more than its fair share of mental space. This essay, then, is an attempt to account for teaching about textiles as an extension of my research, and to think through the successes and failures of a course on Textiles and Activism that I created and taught in 2008. When writing the course, one pedagogical question provided the focus: how could the way that students thought about, used, bought and made textiles be changed? How could I encourage them, to use Sarat Maharaj's lovely phrase, to "think through" textiles?[1] In short, I hoped to encourage students not just to knit, but also to think about what the act of knitting might mean.

CASTING ON: THE UNIVERSITY AND DEPARTMENT

Textiles and Activism took place in a department with two sewing machines and no other equipment—no looms, no knitting machines, no software, not even knitting needles that could be lent to the students. Yet, the course had been advertised as if there could be a studio component. I initially saw this as potentially disastrous, but over the course of the semester, students demonstrated how pervasive and ubiquitous textiles really are. Almost half of them decided to make a studio project in lieu of a final research essay, and in some ways, the material limitations of the class forced self-reflection in a way that might not otherwise have been possible. One student, for example, knitted a winter outfit out of plastic bags and other found materials, another created a series of comic strips about knitting, while a third made paintings that she then embroidered.

previous page LISA ANNE AUERBACH, *Bodycount Mittens*, ongoing
project. Photograph by Lisa Anne Auerbach. Image courtesy the artist.
opposite JERILEA ZEMPEL, *Guns and Rosettes*, Poznan, Poland, 1998.
Russian tank and crochet. Photograph by Jerilea Zempel. Image
courtesy the artist.
above KIRSTY ROBERTSON, Textiles and Activism display in
the hallway of the Visual Arts Building, 2009. Mixed materials,
183 x 914.5 cm. Photograph by Kim Clarke. Image courtesy University
of Western Ontario. © Kim Clarke.

INTERNATIONAL FIBER COLLABORATIVE, *Gas Station Project*, 2007. Photograph by Cathryn Lahm. Image courtesy the artists.

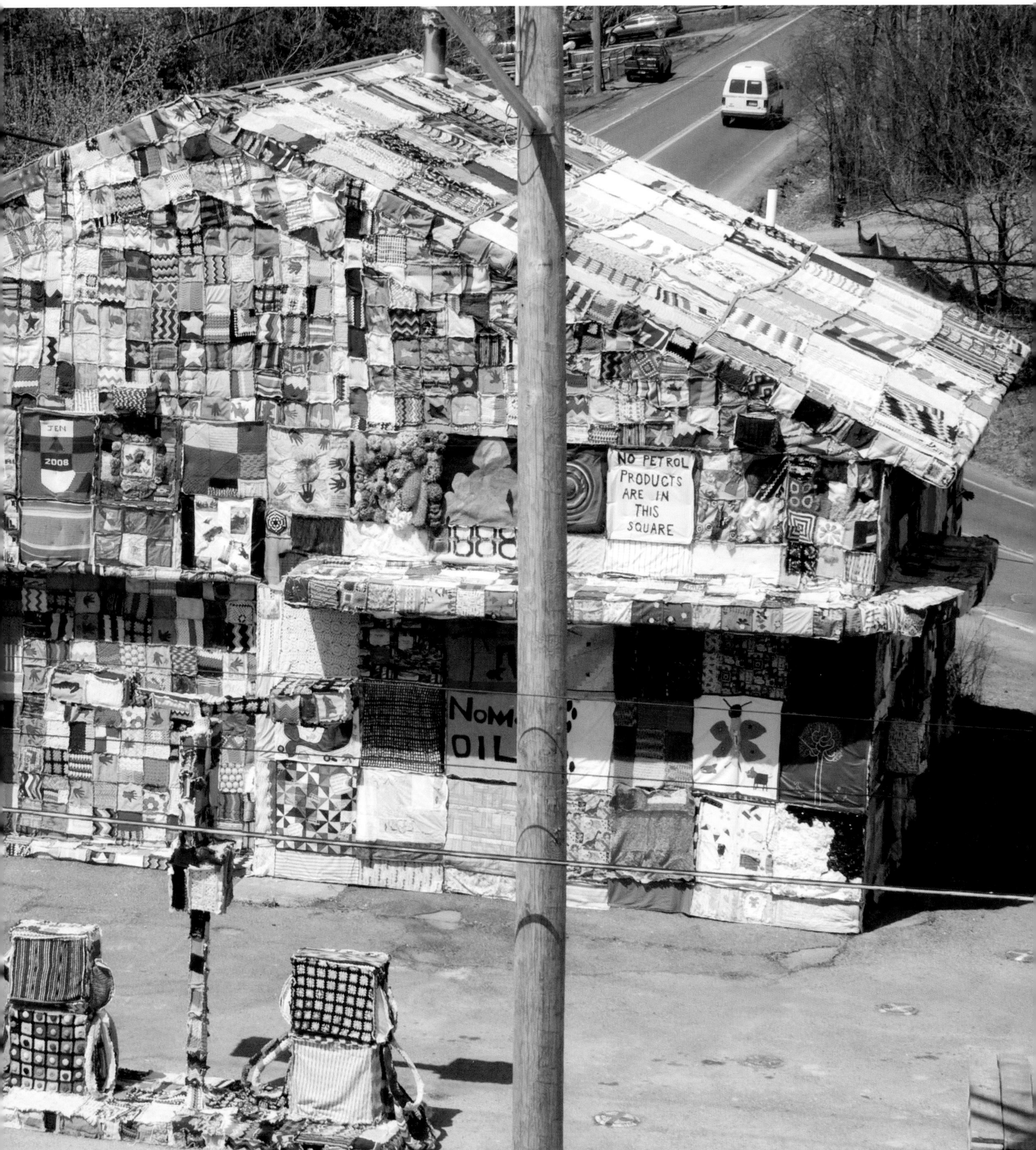
JEN
2008
NO PETROL
PRODUCTS
ARE IN
THIS
SQUARE

Despite the studio limitations, Textiles and Activism drew primarily from students enrolled in Visual Arts degrees, there were only a few exceptions, and although the class was open to all who had the one prerequisite of a foundation course in Art History, the enrollment was entirely female. While this was something of a concern for me, members of the class seemed to be largely unfazed, and in some ways used it to create a safe space in the classroom for the discussion of gender.

The gender imbalance of the class speaks obliquely to an ongoing issue in the teaching, making and display of textiles. At the end of the semester, one student wrote, "before this class I didn't realize it's not only for 'old ladies'."[2] This was, in fact, a difficult stereotype to shake. Throughout the class a number of students noted their surprise at the quantity of contemporary artists using textiles, but also remarked that even as the art world has opened to fibre and craft based arts, traditional techniques are often reframed as design or contemporary art, thereby erasing or at least obscuring female histories of practice.

THE CLASS

Class began with a consideration of Rozsika Parker's seminal text *The Subversive Stitch*, and moved through units on sweatshops, fashion and gender, textiles and postcolonialism, gender and textiles, textiles and technology, and cloth and memory.[3] Activist projects were introduced throughout, including knitting interventions by The Revolutionary Knitting Circle in Canada, and Microrevolt in the United States, collaborative projects such as the International Fiber Collective's *Gas Station Project*, the IKnit UK *Knit a River* for Water Aid, knitted graffiti such as the *Knit Knot Tree* by the jafagirls, as well as projects by artists, such as Jerilea Zemple's *Guns and Rosettes* and Lisa Anne Auerbach's *Body Count Mittens*.

Such projects were contextualised with historical examples, including the suffragists' use of embroidered banners, and the use of knitting by anti-nuclear activists at Greenham Common. The idea was to get students thinking about the ways that textiles and knitting were interpolated in their lives, and how they themselves were connected to a long history of activism, environmental and sweatshop concerns, all profoundly interwoven into today's changing economy.

What I hoped to do with this class was to "sneak activism in". Previously, I have taught courses specifically on activism and art, and have tried to bring an activist agenda to my teaching. But politics in the classroom is a precarious business. Defenses often come up at images of people putting themselves on the line for a political cause. Non-mainstream opinions tend to be described and dismissed as "biased", and the status quo is often vigorously defended even as those defending it describe themselves as different, unique and politically-aware. In their article "Teaching Eighties Babies Sixties Sensibilities," Georgina Hickey and Peggy Hargis outline some of the difficulties of teaching about collective action and social change to a generation that seems to be largely uninterested. The article outlines their frustrations with students "unwilling or unable to recognise the workings of power, privilege, and inequality in their own lives".[4] Those who most enjoy the benefits of privilege, the two authors note, are also those least likely to see the systemic structures and rampant inequalities keeping that privilege in place. Certainly, my own experience with teaching activism has largely, though not entirely, mirrored this thinking.[5]

I was banking strongly on the perception of textiles as ultimately non-threatening and distinctly familiar, in order to stage a *détournement* of my own—to use, in other words, the very stereotypes associated with textiles to keep defenses down. In doing this I borrowed strongly from a number of activist projects that similarly use knitting to contrast the pacifism of protesters with the violence of the state or forces of security.[6] Thus, although the study of textiles offers a rich history steeped in politics, I suspected that knitting needles would not hold the same kind of threat for students who reacted so strongly against placards, strikes, and tear gas. And perhaps having an awareness of the politics of cloth might bleed into other areas for those who may not have been politically interested or motivated to begin with. For this reason, the class was designed from the start to play on the kind of comfort that students might already have with textiles.

Following a project done by Canadian artist Janet Morton at the Canadian Museum of Civilization, titled *A Crafty Garden*, students began the class by transforming the seminar room into a complete mess in order to create a colourful garden of flowers, made from used sweaters and junk that people had lying around. A great deal of it admittedly came from my basement, but a number of students brought in jars of buttons, sparkles, pipecleaners and used clothing. Although several students admitted at the end that they had been somewhat anxious, fearing that their flowers would be ugly or not good enough, the main goal of the project was successful in breaking down the intimidating space of the seminar classroom, and in introducing students to one another as they discussed a series of questions based on the introductory readings.

If the first class was about community building, the second class was about building trust. This was the final week before I turned control of the class over to the students who would, from this point, create group presentations based on the readings. For this class, students prepared two things: first, they looked at their favourite outfit to see where the various items had come from and what they were made of, and second, they brought in a textile, a term that was not defined, that was of great personal significance to them. As students pulled their items out of their bags, they noted that they often developed relationships with garments, hated to part with them, or infused them with memories of particular events or people. Students brought in a hand-made bag that had been someone's first sewing project, a wrap that had been given by a much-beloved grandmother, a scarf

previous page JAFAGIRLS, *Knit Knot Tree, Xenia Avenue, Yellow Springs, Ohio*, 2007.
Photograph by Corrine Bayraktaroglu. Image courtesy the artists.
opposite JANET MORTON, *A Crafty Garden*, Canadian Museum of Civilization, 2007.
Photograph by Kirsty Robertson.
above IKNIT AND WATERAID, *Knit a River action*, 2006. Photograph by Kirsty Robertson.

that belonged to a boyfriend, a baby-blanket, and a pair of socks that one of the students had been wearing when her father left for the final time.

I suspect that this exercise might have been as important for me as it was for the class. Rarely in our teaching do we come to know our students as individuals. Hickey and Hargis describe the learning process that came about through critically analysing their own behaviour in the classroom and the ways in which, for them, teaching about power and privilege was occasionally undermined by the hierarchical positioning of the teacher at the front of the class imparting information to an expectant audience. Not doing this was an important component of the Textiles and Activism class, but in something as simple as the trust building exercise it quickly became apparent how authority is established in the classroom in seemingly benign ways.

After the two community and trust building exercises, the class really began, opening with a consideration of the history and current day operation of sweatshops, and leading into units on gender, memory and technology, each grounded with examples of artists working within those fields. Every unit was presented to the class by a group of four to five students, who often continued the interactivity of the initial assignments in their presentations. In the class on sweatshops, for example, audience members were asked to perform menial tasks—making knots in string—throughout the presentation. At the end of the class, one of the presenters gathered up all of the knotted pieces of string, on which students had been working for over an hour, and emphatically threw them in the garbage bin, literally 'wasting' the labour of their fellow classmates.

SUBVERSIVE TEACHING

The goal with the Textiles and Activism class was to engage with Jane A Rinehart's term "subversive teaching", which she defines as a style of teaching that "aims to communicate an 'oppositional imagination': an ability to think past received habits of thought and action".[7] Learning takes place within a destabilised learning space—one in which "authority is dispersed", and where "the classroom [is constructed] as a public space in which serious conversations take place about society, culture, politics, and responsibilities".[8]

The limits of the classroom to act as a site where boundaries are pushed, however, were clearly demonstrated by one student who wrote in her response essay:

It made me wonder how many other classroom discussions we have that are not followed through in real life. We discuss buying locally made clothes and exploring the history behind brands we support, but how many people in our class will actually make an effort to do that? Our class brings important issues such as these to light every week and we desire a societal change, but if even our class doesn't 'practice what they preach', what hope does the rest of our society have to change?

There was a certain ease with which the production of textiles could be about someone else and somewhere else, while the gender dimensions of the production of hand-made textiles and craft in the West tended to be seen as separate. Women knitting in North America, for example, were often discussed as if they were completely disconnected from those working in factories in China, Honduras or India.

In the feedback summaries students wrote at the end of the class, the vast network of sweatshops, and the alternatives to sweated labour were noted as the most important things that students had learned. Articles by Lou Cabeen, Maureen Sherlock and Alan Howard in the book *The Object of Labor: Art, Cloth and Cultural Production* were repeatedly mentioned as having been the most influential, in addition to the films *China Blue*, *Mardi Gras: Made in China*, and *The Hidden Face of Globalization*, excerpts of which we watched in class. Further, Andrew Ross's book *No Sweat*, with its detailing of the numerous sweatshops in Los Angeles and the El Monte case forced students to look at their own backyards. Students brought in their own examples of locally made clothing, and stories of how their favourite clothing companies had begun to outsource manufacturing.

In one case, a student told of her grandmother whose personal experience of extremely poor labour conditions in a textile factory in London, Ontario, in the 1960s, only blocks from where the class was taking place, collapsed the distance between the documentaries we were watching and the possibility that such conditions might exist in Canada. The ownership of Value Village, an extremely popular thriftstore chain, by the much-maligned Walmart became a touchstone throughout, as did the fact that LuluLemon, a very popular Canadian manufacturer of yoga and exercise clothing, had recently transferred some of its production to China.

This was a difficult unit to balance, as in North America, prejudice is growing against goods "Made in China" in a manner that hints at an underlying xenophobia and fear aimed at the rise of China as an economic power. It was difficult to explain the, minor, Canadian role in setting up the conditions, whereby, a national Canadian textile industry could be allowed to decline as part and parcel of Canada's ongoing support of the liberalization of trade. Students tended to subscribe to what they were hearing in the media, often overlooking the consumption end of the equation. Thus, although I believe the class was successful in fostering a knowledge of the extremes of abuse, environmental and labour, in the textile industry, I think it was less successful in creating an awareness of how each of us is implicated in the circulations of goods that bring those inequalities into being.[9]

At the end of the class, on the day when I, with the help of two students, taught the class how to knit, I asked students to reflect on what textiles meant to them, and on what they had learned in the class. As they struggled to master knit and purl stitches, students reflected that textiles are something that can be understood by everyone. One student noted that because material is tactile it can be used and be useful.

Another wrote, "One can seem intelligent and skilled", while someone else noted, "I think that textile creation is a gendered activity but rather than that being [a] bad [thing] it creates a positive discursive space." Another student, struggling to master the stitches, wrote: "I was worried that I would fail the class horribly because I am pathetic at knitting", before noting that she had actually come to appreciate understanding the way in which her clothing was made.

When I teach this class again in the future, I would like to draw even further on what Gerald Shenk and David Takacs call "praxis pedagogy".[10] In their words, this means finding ways for students to connect their learning to their everyday lives, primarily through praxis, action and collaborative work. The process described by Shenk and Takacs involves repeated self-reflection, or, as they put it, "Each new praxis cycle should make students more thoughtful, ethical, and effective citizens, whose public and private acts are informed by a more sophisticated and self-reflective understanding of the disciplines they are studying."[11]

In hindsight, this was an extremely fun class to teach. The combination of studio and academic work, even without proper equipment, was a rewarding one, and I think that students from both sides of the department, studio and art history, felt comfortable with that. As an activist, it was more difficult to tell. The mere title of the course gave students an idea of what was expected, and it was difficult to tell where my politics ended and their ideas began. But I do think a number of them joined the department's knitting club....

QUIET ACTIVISM

DEIRDRE NELSON

This is the recipe for my craft:

- Find a location, a text, or a humorous story.
- Study relevant people.
- Find a contemporary link.
- Develop an idea and study a traditional technique.
- Add a bit of humour.
- And some craftsmanship and hand skills.
- And translate into something tangible, which will be inclusive, engaging and encourage a smile.

Much of my work combines social and textile history, and retells stories relating to places where knitting is embedded into culture and history. Recently, research in locations such as Shetland and Uist have provided many stories and inspiration for exhibited textile works. While working with these communities I have become interested in quiet activism in the form of knitting groups who work quietly for a variety of charity projects. Those working do not consider themselves artists or crafts people and are not part of the fashionable 'craft-activism' movement, but possess fine traditional skills and have been working in this less overt manner for some time now. Each small piece of knitting that is created joins others to make something larger, for the good of another community.

previous page DEIRDRE NELSON, *Salmon, Mackeral, Herring*, 2008. Harris wool, gold embroidery, 40 x 50 cm. Photograph by Shannon Tofts.

left DEIRDRE NELSON, *Life Jacket*, 2005. Life jacket, wool ripped from fisherman's gansey, 80 x 40 cm. Exhibited in Dangers of Sewing and Knitting, 2005. Photograph by Andy Stark. Image courtesy the artist. © Andy Stark.

opposite Deirdre Nelson knitting fish. Photograph by Steve Carter.

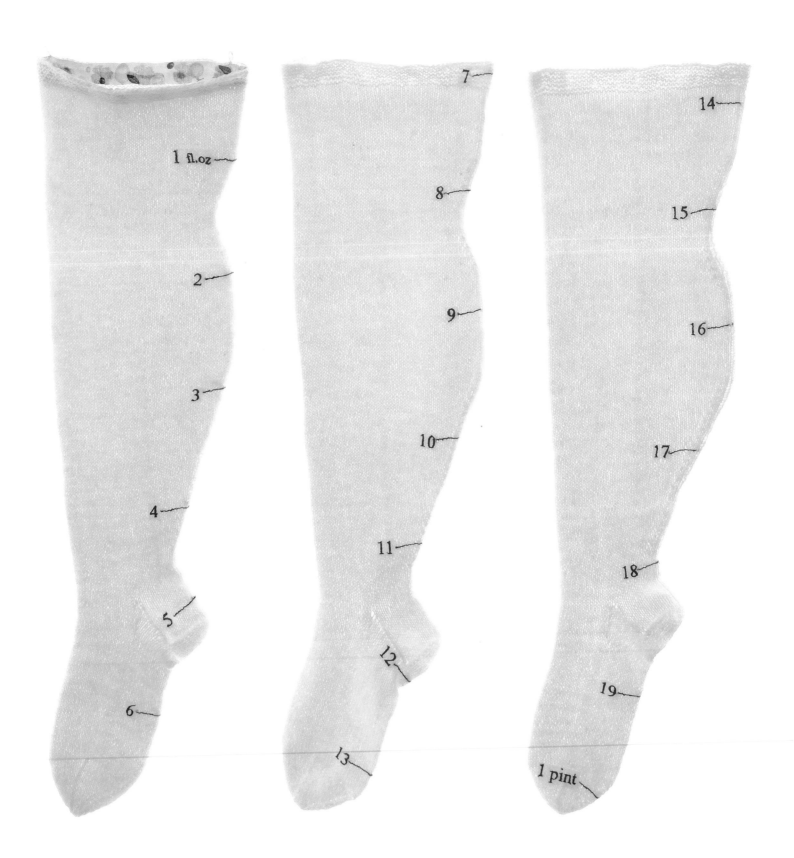

opposite DEIRDRE NELSON, *Gin Socks*, 2005. Shetland wool, transfer print, silk, 90 x 90 cm. Photograph by Mark Sinclair. Image courtesy the artist. © Mark Sinclair.
above DEIRDRE NELSON, *Multi Tasking*, 2008. Shovel and wool, 150 x 45 cm. Photograph by Olwen Shone. Image courtesy the artist.

below DEIRDRE NELSON, *Kale Spoon*, 2008. Wool and silk,
30 x 12 cm. Photograph by Olwen Shone. Image courtesy
the artist.
opposite DEIRDRE NELSON, *Hair sleeve*, 2007. Shetland
wool, human hair, 50 x 30 cm. Photograph by Billy Fox.
Image courtesy the artist. © Billy Fox.

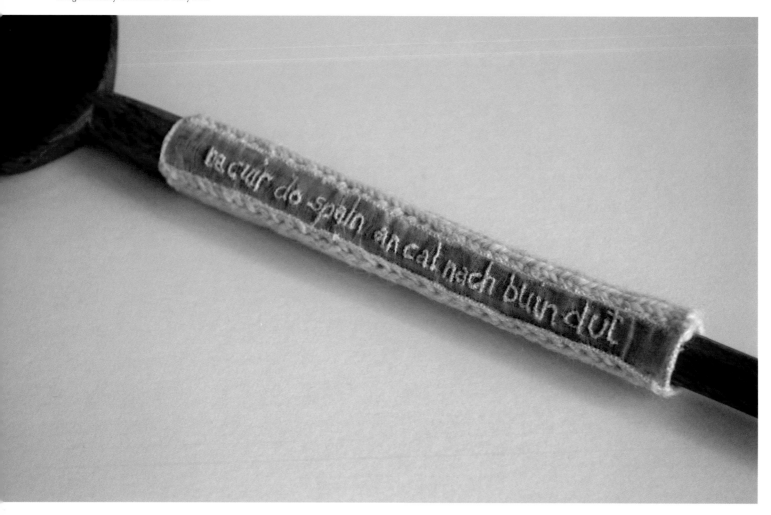

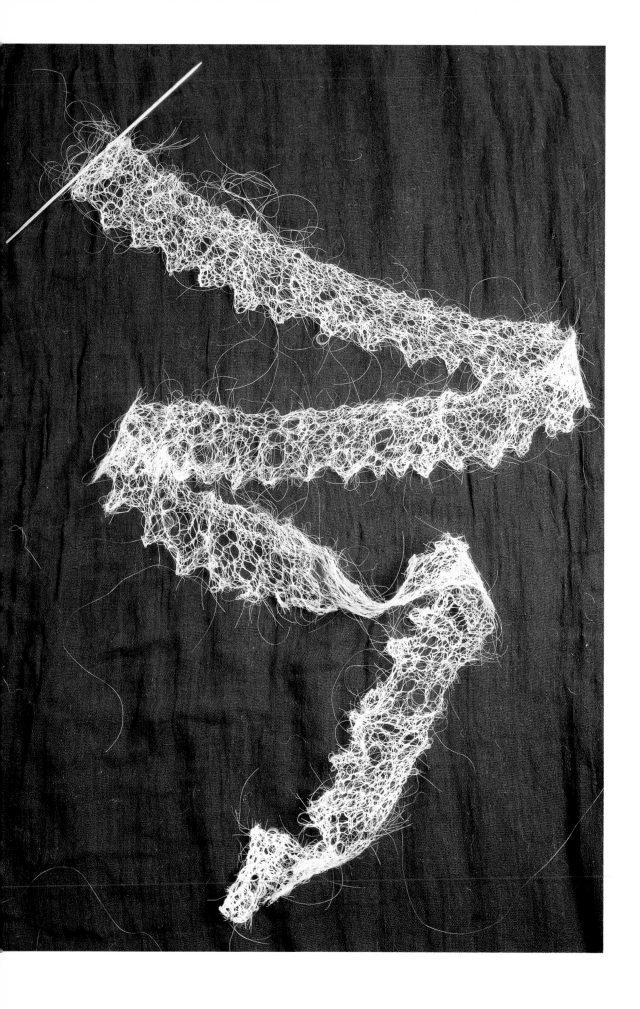

KNITTING NATION

LIZ COLLINS

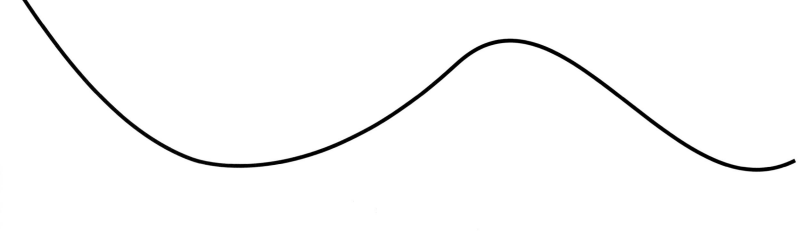

KNITTING NATION is an ongoing, collaborative performance and site-specific installation project created by artist/designer Liz Collins. It explores aspects of textile and apparel manufacturing, laying bare the process of making machine knitted fabric. The project functions as a commentary on how humans interact with machines, global manufacturing, trade and labour, iconography, and fashion.

This photo essay shows the fourth and fifth *KNITTING NATION* events and pieces. *KNITTING NATION Phase 4: PRIDE* paid homage to the original gay pride rainbow flag by reconstructing it. The rainbow pride flag was originally designed and constructed by Gilbert Baker in San Francisco in 1978 to symbolise the diversity of the gay community, with each colour carrying specific meaning. It has now become an internationally recognised icon of Lesbian Gay Bisexual Transgender and Queer communities, politics and/or market-based identities. *KNITTING NATION Phase 4: PRIDE* brought attention to this important and controversial symbol, examining and reflecting on it, in the midst of the Rhode Island Pride Festival in June of 2008, where rainbow flags were everywhere. The giant knitted piece

made on that day has since been exhibited as an object, installed in spaces in different draped and blob-like configurations, and has functioned for the artist as an accurate commentary on her own complex feelings about the rainbow flag.

KNITTING NATION Phase 5: RISD by Design was created for the inauguration of a new Rafael Moneo designed building in Providence, Rhode Island in the fall of 2008. The site provided was the rooftop of a seven storey, historical building in the heart of Providence that faced the shiny new structure made of brick with a silver metal finish. The piece was a playful response to the new building, containing dozens of silver mylar balloons that hovered over the surface of the piece, quivering in the wind. The lengths of knit yardage were zip-tied, rather than stitched together, which brought the scalloped seam, one of Collins' signature garment construction techniques, into the piece on a large-scale. The piece grew and became strangely sexy and jewel-like, and for three days, the building looked like it was wearing an exquisite piece of embellished lingerie.

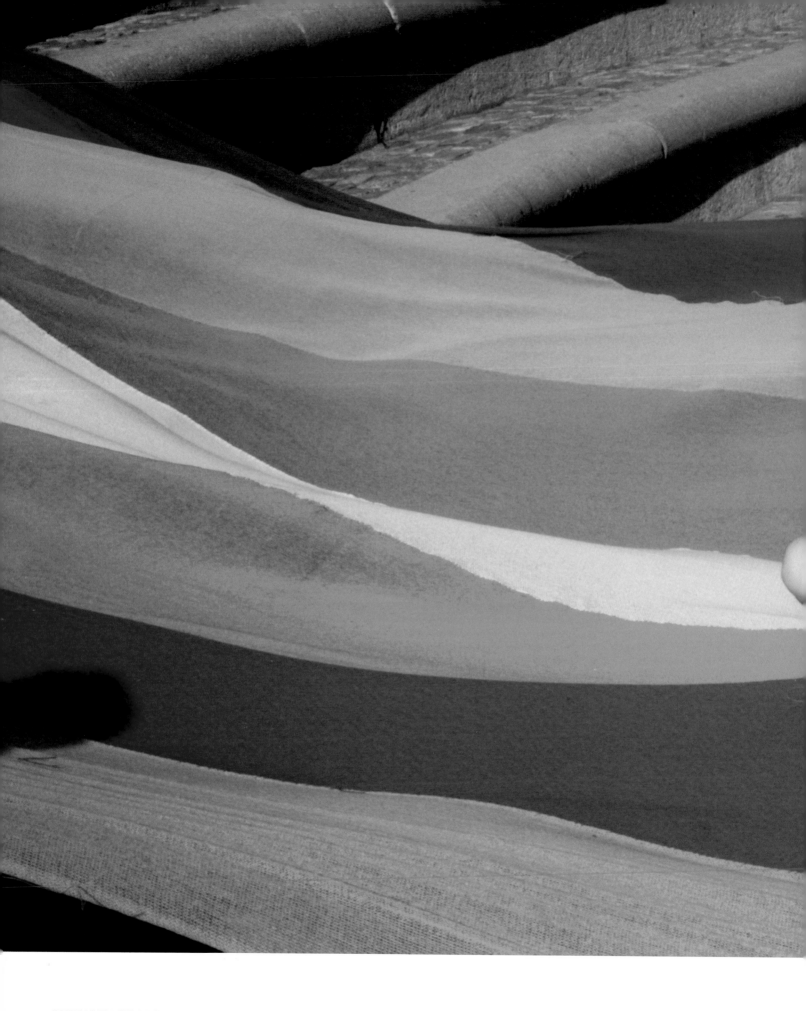

previous page and left LIZ COLLINS, *Knitting Nation Phase 4: Pride*, 2008. A site specific, multi-media, time-based installation at Waterplace Park in Providence, Rhode Island. Cotton yarn, dimensions variable. Photograph by Delia Kovack. Image courtesy the artist.

below and opposite LIZ COLLINS, *Knitting Nation Phase 5: RISD by Design*, 2008. A site specific, multi-media, time-based installation at the RISD Museum at Rhode Island School of Design. Rayon and cotton yarn, zip ties, mylar balloons, dimensions variable. Photograph by Brian James. Image courtesy the artist.

THREAT IN THE LANDSCAPE?

SOPHIE HORTON

I am interested in how textiles occupy the external environment and the effect their presence has on our understanding of site. Can a colourful knitted site-specific artwork alter an apparently fixed urban or rural landscape in a meaningful way? Can a temporary installation survive in the viewer's memory?

Commissioning bodies often envisage textile interventions as temporary. I see time as significant to our understanding of installation art. It takes time to see how an art intervention situates itself to its site and settles. Several of my 'temporary' knitted works have stayed on view for up to a year beyond the original time scale.

I am also interested in challenging our preconceptions of materials. Context, site, or form of an object can alter interpretations. For example, wool, acrylic and cotton yarns are often associated with domesticity. When displaced from this familiar environment into an industrial or agricultural setting, viewers are surprised to discover that my installations are not metal mesh, but a knitted soft fabric.

It fascinates me that knitted woollen, acrylic and lurex interventions can appear as a threat in the landscape. A Ministry of Defence site is adjacent to Cove Park, where I was artist in residence. The Ministry of Defence frequently visited me whilst I was stitching on fencing to create *Cordon*, maybe linking my practice to the Greenham Common women's peace camp—at Greenham Common, protesters sewed visual objections onto the fencing where the Trident missiles were housed. While I did not share these intentions of overt protest, I sensed the perception of threat that my knitting provoked.

I relish creating barriers that through location, metaphor and history, persuade us that textiles is a force to be reckoned with.

SOPHIE HORTON, *Cordon*, Cove Park, Scotland, 2004. Locally
sourced lambswool, shetland wool and acrylic wool and lurex,
400 m long. Photograph by Ruth Clarke.

opposite SOPHIE HORTON, *Cordon*, Cove Park, Scotland, 2004. Locally sourced lambswool, shetland wool and acrylic wool and lurex, 400 m long. Photograph by Ruth Clarke.
below SOPHIE HORTON, *Charge Over The Fence*, Bolwick Hall, Norfolk, 2003. Acrylic wool, wool and fencing, 1.5 x 66 m. Image courtesy the artist.

SOPHIE HORTON, *Live Wire*, 2004. Acrylic wool, wire, 1 x 47 m.
Cove Park, Scotland. Photograph by Ruth Clarke.

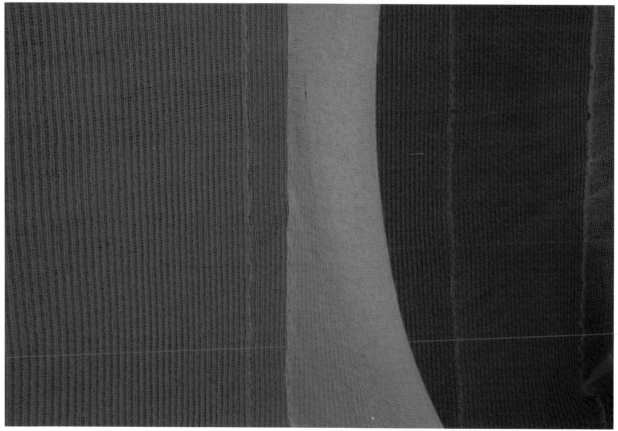

opposite top and bottom SOPHIE HORTON, *Red Back*, 2006.
Knitted acrylic wool and wooden pergola, 3.5 x 7 x 3 m.
Photograph by George Merrick.
top and bottom SOPHIE HORTON, *Safety Net*, 2007.
Cotton, acrylic and wool, 8.5 x 4.5 m. Courtesy the artist.

above and opposite SOPHIE HORTON, *Eye Candy*, 2005. Crocheted acrylic wool, 12 m x 6 cm x 1 cm. Illinois State University, Normal, Illinois USA. Image Courtesy the artist.

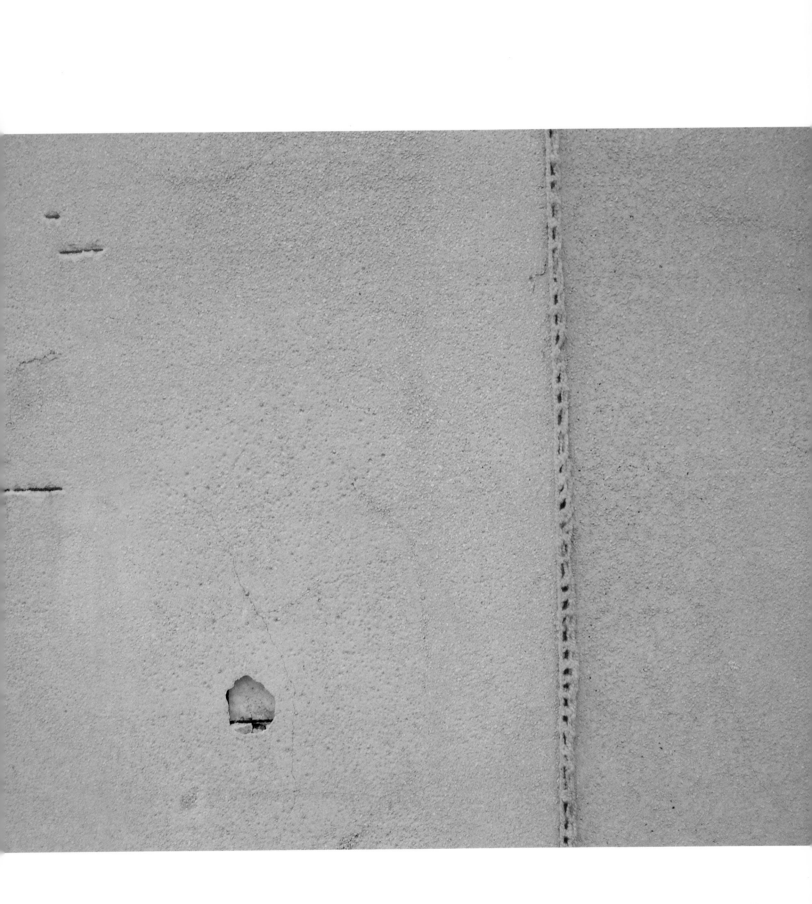

ENCOUNTERING 'THE BOGEY':
THE SEPARATE—BUT—PARALLEL (AND NON-MERCENARY) CULTS OF CRAFTIVISM AND UNSENTIMENTAL WANTON SEXUALITY, POST-2001

LYCIA TROUTON

Our imaginations—the best thing about being human—are becoming atrophied, and difference is off the agenda... Now there are three movies, two chords and no choice.[1]

A recent heightened anxiety about the self's connection with 'The Other', and the necessity of a culturally diverse material world has driven artists to Craftivism. Since the introduction of the internet and the mid-1990s digital age, when the screen took over real-time relations and touch, Western conceptual craftivists have rebelled against time management, efficient production and previously defined parameters of women's appropriate behaviour.[2] In this essay, I discuss the importance of Craftivism hitting real-time public space at the same time as another worldwide cult phenomena, also led by female artists/artisans/creative types, occurred: the frank sex-memoire.[3] The cult of Craftivism/Knitted Graffiti/Yarn Bombing began about the same time as the *entrée* of Internet Sex-Blogging in 2004. Both movements are anonymous, non-consumer oriented, and are about the body, touch and an unyieldingness in the face of fear—'fear' is personified by the rhetorical character of 'The Bogey' or 'Entity'. This essay's focus is on the post-internet era 'embodied' and 'encoded' creative communication strategy of a particularly eccentric artist/craftivist, known as Rozzi George, from Darwin, Australia.

Women diarists and textile artists have always shared something in common: the discussion of how their intimate lives intersect with their public and political views. The 'best practice' of both post-feminist cult movements, Craftivism and the sex-blog, is, in other words, what I would call: "a Playful Pranksterness".[4]

I present the following list of 'best practice' Craftivism in Public Space. In doing so, I acknowledge how the cult of Craftivism, has and, can continue to piggyback on the cult of the post-2001 Sex Memoire, with gracious kindness and thanks to the highly respected French art critic and infamous sexual memoire writer, Catherine Millet, with assistance from the uncompromisingly weird Jessica Berens.[5]

· Wear a black or dull coloured, sober minded cardigan.
· Consider yourself a part of the intelligensia or intellectual set.

• Do not launch yourself from a 1960s, 1970s or 1980s feminist or political springboard, but a post-feminist 2001 era.

• Do not conform to the mould "that contemporary culture has created to define, and incarcerate, a woman's sexuality".[6]

• Revel in your extraordinary freedom of playfully enjoying being 'above disgust' whether as a craftivist or as a sexual libertine.

• Speak about either sexuality or domestic duties with completely direct, unrelenting frankness and unsentimental openness. Do not tolerate the sentimental or romantic or 'retro'.

• Do not flirt with nor rely upon a pretty or cute youthfulness or sexiness.

• Be an excessively reserved player.

• Do not engage in conspicuous consumerism nor negotiations of 'mercenary relationships'.

• Do not establish an empathy between your reader/viewer and your work—your pornographic writing or Craftivism.

• Whatever age you are, act over 45 or 55 in your level of wisdom, r.e. an empowered worldliness about sexuality and knowledge of contemporary art.

For the first time in history, après the 1970s pill, après the 1980s HIV virus safe sex/silence=death scare, and après the advent of e-social networking/dating via the internet, women bloggers began speaking incredibly frankly about 'wanton carnal' sexual desires, now without risk of pregnancy or sharing of diseases. Catherine Millet and various bloggers are working from a long tradition of published female authors and bohemian, erotic diarists dating back to the likes of Anne Desclos (1950s), who worked under a pseudonym, Anaïs Nin (1940s), and Kate Chopin (1890s).[7] With the most recent cult-wave, the post 2001 co-ed world was flabbergasted that women would freely express such basic instinctual drives and callousness, but fellow sisters came out of the closet in droves, feeling more connected and seemingly empowered than ever. The invention of the internet had provided anonymity, and therefore safety, that women throughout history have needed in order to explore and expose a different side of their personalities. The cult following, which developed with Web 2.0 technology has made for a startlingly rapid growth of readership.

At the same time, albeit on a very different subject matter, previously silent and dutiful Craftivist Knitters spilled out of their quiet wallflower corner perches and into the streets. This genre of women were not, perhaps as is the perception of the Sex Blogger, 'callous and carefree', but were/are seen as 'concerned, committed carer-citizens', whether or not they had an independent-minded sexual life or a committed life partner. These Public Art Craftivists entered plazas and architectonic spaces, not with their sedate knitting and crocheting or needlework projects touting patronising innocuous sentiments, but sporting various emphatic politicised statements through their

metaphoric yarn bombs about various social ills. In Australia, such Craftivists have proved to be concerned with pollution and old-growth forest destruction, industrial farming practices and inhumane farming/fast-food packaging practices.

The post-internet era of the creative Craftivist communication strategy by women public artists can express gratitude, in part, to the female sex blogger for her newly found public freedom and the acceptance/tolerance of the genre of Knitted Graffiti or Yarn Bombing in unlicensed public spaces.

What both groups of creative women have in common is that they seem to be independently minded 'operators' in their public life, all the while still choosing to be either anonymous, and/or safety conscious, in either real-time or on the internet. Both movements were/are a type of underground genre about the body through encoded forms of communication. The latter group might seem to be a little more genteel and charitable than the former group of Sex Blogger narcissists! The sex blogger's work is accomplished by a less 'embodied' means of purpose—text—because of her primary use of the keyboard and screen, than the knitter/Yarn Bomber who is more engaged with a hands-on textile arts practice.

Marina Warner's book *No Go the Bogeyman* is about myths of the cultural exploration of fear, comfort and our ambiguous amusement with scare tactics through a discussion of ogres and child guzzlers in popular fiction. I purport that both groups were/are dealing with the real or metaphoric 'Knitted Bogey', a monster that, according to Warner, gives us clues to our moral compass in society as it represents the "engineering of hatred" and, thus, shows us our fears as expressed in a "large, distorted glass".[8]

'Knitted Entities' or 'Bogeys', such as those created by Craftivist installation artist-performer Rozzi George, who lives between Darwin, Australia and Yogyakarta, Indonesia, address our human desire for warmth, comfort, nurturance and intimate connection. Like Marina Warner, George is considering and critiquing the concept of 'fear' in a world of globalised terrorism where violence has spread and been normalised. The 'Bogey' also reminds us and, in a *double entendre*, conveys the very opposites of these things: repulsion, especially of the body and the maternal nurturer, and, therefore, fear.

Knitting, playful and poverty-stricken a medium though it is, is in the process of being historicised into the high art mainstream. While the wool industry in Australia has been immortalised in infamous poetry about The Shearer, such as in well-known poetry of AB 'Banjo' Patterson, at the other end of the production-line spectrum, the domestic labourer, the one who knits is still in need of attention.

Currently an installation performance artist, Rozzi George's career has included public artist—mosaic ceramic tile work —interior designer, gallery owner, and importer/exporter of Indonesian art. Her 2005 diary entry about her installation *Terra Alienius*—a direct reference to, and subversive critique of the phrase "Terra Nullius"—notes:

The knitted striations of earthly, coloured yarns, when they folded into the hills and valleys, reminded me of a landscape. I placed some of the toy characters

ENCOUNTERING 'THE BOGEY': THE SEPARATE—BUT—PARALLEL (AND NON-MERCENARY) CULTS OF CRAFTIVISM AND UNSENTIMENTAL WANTON SEXUALITY, POST-2001

107

and stuffed mittens in the landscape and imagined narratives that were inevitable.

There was once a sacred land that shimmered with joyful brilliance. But imposters came and brought strange plants and animals with them. The landscape quickly faded as the earth itself was drained of its spirit by bad farming practices. The plants, like the preposterous prickly pear, known in Indonesia as 'Pinocchio's Nose', took over and the poor, imported animals were forced to eat all the sparkling native vegetation. They also gave the local animals illnesses....

Things became so dire that, even from outer space, the once sacred shimmery land looked stark and stricken.... Thinking it looked an easy place to colonise, some passing aliens came and claimed it for themselves. They renamed it Terra Alienius.

They killed the fatted sheep and an amazing giant rabbit that had been genetically modified and cloned so much it had developed a growth disorder, on whose back the previous coloniser had ridden, and took it back to their leader.

From this image of the Australian landscape, George knitted a series of life-sized alter egos that explore notions of comfort and fear through 'The Bogey' or 'Knitted Entity' —'Entity' is the artist's preferred term, my preferred term is after Marina Warner: 'Bogey'. *SuperKnitWit 1: An Outrageously Outspoken Art Critic: PostModernism Ate My Baby* is a headless, human-sized doll wearing a size 26 sweater. The work's text is a reference to René Magritte's calligram *This is Not a Pipe*, 1926, and is conceived for a landscape where global terrorism, internet sex blogging and soft porn, by both men and women, is the 'new norm'.

No longer able to comfort the world with her super heroism, this menopausal doll woman, who in a previous incarnation was an outrageously outspoken art critic, was 'murdered'. The artist then 'cremated' her ' '/'Knitted Entity', after the installation was vandalised at the University art gallery, and filmed the ceremony at the oceanside of Fannie Bay Beach, Darwin, later shown as part of a further installation on DVD at 24 Hour Art alternative artspace in Darwin. So the myth goes....

In Memoriam.
Superknitwit.
Birthdate unknown—died 11 November 2006.
Artist and art activist.
Mother and partner.
Superheroine.

We are devastated to announce the sudden and tragic death of Superknitwit. Treasured figment of an artist's imagination, cherished wife of adorable, and well endowed, Scroman, beloved, adoring and devoted mother of Cardie, Beanie, Jumpie and Installation, she will be sadly missed.

On 11 November 2005, she was the victim of a brutal attack, cold bloodedly decapitated and stabbed in the heart with a knitting needle by an unknown cowardly and vicious assailant—you know who you are, curse you and your ignorance.

As an art activist and obsessed knitter she dared to challenge the conventions of canonised art and questioned the status quo of acceptable artistic mediums. She became a superhero fighting for justice for the knitted object and smashed the trope of the mild mannered knitting housewife. As a fun loving, unconventional woman, it's a shame her efforts were sometimes not only misunderstood but obviously stirred viciousness in the hearts of some. So, as deeply unfortunate as it is, it transpired that, just as she lived by the knitting needle, so she died by the knitting needle.

In a very private ceremony she was cremated on Fannie Bay Beach on 2 May 2006. She has gone to meet her maker and to celebrate her life and commemorate her untimely passing we would like, in loving memory, to offer those of you who remember her fondly a chance to share the grief of her family and friends and fans. We therefore present this record of that burning ceremony. It's what she would have wanted.

No flowers please—unless they're knitted.
A saintly superhero now an angel she will live in our hearts forever. May she rest in knitted peace. Ave Superknitwit.

After the disappearance of 'The Bogey'... "human society, culture and law begin".[9]

Female artists-craftivists may, indeed, help shape civilisation away from the fearful 11 September 2001-era ghost 'Bogey' dramas, of the complex issues of fear/hatred and power hungry abominations against society's well being, to put warm, fuzzy "kindliness" in place.[10] For example, now monogamous, even the promiscuous Catherine M has since admitted to needing simple embodied affection in her life.[11] Craftivists, and less directly sex bloggers, are creating a new climate in society where caring is cool and independence of mind and body is respected, unfettered from strictures on women's behaviour, which hearken back to the Victorian and Edwardian eras, and the prankster is rewarded for her courage in the concept of play.

ROZZI GEORGE, *Tree Cosies*, 2006. Plain knitting, 3 m height x 50 cm diameter. The bottom of the other side of the Tree Cosy states 'Terra Alienius'. People's choice award: sculpture-in-the-park, Darwin Arts Festival, Darwin, Australia. Photograph by Rozzi George. Image courtesy Rozzi George.

ENCOUNTERING 'THE BOGEY': THE SEPARATE—BUT—PARALLEL (AND NON-MERCENARY) CULTS OF CRAFTIVISM AND UNSENTIMENTAL WANTON SEXUALITY, POST-2001

109

opposite ROZZI GEORGE, *Superknitwit I: An Outrageously Outspoken Art Critic: Postmodernism Ate My Baby*, 2005. Plain knitting, 120 x 90–170 x 275 cm, with a size 26 sweater. Detail of 'Knitted Entity', or 'Bogey', which doubles as a performative doll-puppet-self-portrait. The artist or an interactive viewer can sit behind the installation sculpture and place their head 'behind' the sweater for a photo opportunity. Photograph by Rozzi George. Image courtesy Rozzi George.

below ROZZI GEORGE, *Superknitwit III: Terra Alienius*, 2005. Plain knitting, 120 x 90–170 x 275 cm, with a size 26 sweater. 'Knitted Entity', or 'Bogey', which doubles as a performative doll-puppet-self-portrait. This artwork-installation was later transformed into 'Tree Cosy' for art-in-the-park. Photograph by Rozzi George. Image courtesy Rozzi George.

CRAFT, QUEERNESS, AND GUERILLA TACTICS:

AN EXTENDED MAKER'S STATEMENT

LACEY JANE ROBERTS

Knitting and textiles were the last fields that I ever thought I'd be in. I wanted to be a welder, woodworker, or writer. However, through a series of accidents I've found knitting to be a potent and provocative agent to break down constructed categories of material and visual culture.

My knitting is rooted in two words: queer and craft. Both queer and craft are very tricky words. They both have many definitions and can communicate so many different ideas that they are almost, if not impossible, to define. Many find this ambiguity difficult and problematic. I find it fierce and beautiful.

Craft is all over the place—it represents everything from exquisite artisan objects to kitschy handmade trinkets, to the hip and cute items produced in today's trendy DIY culture. Queer is most often used to describe a non-normative identity—the configurations of gender, race, sexuality, class, etc. that are viewed as 'Other'. Besides being difficult to define, craft and queer mirror each other in another way—they exist in the margins and are often categorised as occupying 'low' spaces in the hierarchical structure of visual and material culture. My knitting embraces the low and amateur to queer craft and in turn makes craft a manifestation of my queerness.

I use knitting to break down the classifications of art, craft, design and architecture in an attempt to thwart the categorisation of my practice. Maintaining a hybrid practice is a manifestation of my own queer identity. For me knitting is the queerest media there is. Knitting complicates the linear and the two needles activate a third space illustrated by the materiality created by knitting. Just when you think you've pinned knitting down someone, or something, finds a new way to queer it.

I've always been drawn to installation art because it envelopes me. Not only can I view the art, but to an extent I can literally be in the art. Knitting one stitch at a time is a pain-staking process, but using this technique to create a large, interactive installation was a challenge I wanted to take on. My first large knitted installation, *Dropping Stitches*, is a knitted poem you can walk through. Each letter is mismatched in colour and hand knitted. It was shown with a video of my hands stitching, emphasising labour and the feminist act of intergenerational skill sharing, which I view as an act of love.

After completing my undergraduate studies I applied to Master of Fine Arts programmes to further explore the link between knitting and fine art. During the application process I received a letter from California College of Arts and Crafts announcing that the school, effective immediately, would be known as California College of the Arts. 'Crafts' would no longer be part of the title. This change came in the wake of several other prominent institutions that also erased 'craft/s' from their name, beginning with the American

previous page LACEY JANE ROBERTS, *We couldn't get in. We couldn't get out.*, 2006–2007. Crank-knit yarn, hand-woven wire, steel poles, assorted hardware, 25.5 x 76 cm. Image courtesy the artist.
left and opposite LACEY JANE ROBERTS, *The Master's Tools (decay goes both ways)*, 2008. Crank-knit yarn, hand-woven wire, steel poles, assorted hardware, 23 x 38 cm x variable dimensions. Image courtesy the artist.

Craft Museum, which changed its name to Museum of Arts and Design. While various reasons were given for dropping the word 'craft', the many negative stereotypes associated with the word craft were most often cited for its deletion. The stereotypes were too much for institutions to tackle and it became easier to nix craft rather than recontextualise it. It seemed to me to be the right time for another guerilla installation. *& Crafts* was installed at dawn, 3 April 2005, on the facade of the California College of the Arts' San Francisco Campus during the morning of MFA open studios. Knitted in glowing neon orange yarn, the piece remained on the front of the school for a week. The reaction of the students, faculty and staff was overwhelmingly positive and sometimes bordered on ecstatic. Most people at CCA were unequivocally loyal and attached to 'crafts'. The communications department was a little less thrilled. I did not know that they were filming the promotional video for the school the day after I installed. Needless to say, I ruined a pivotal shot.

The second year of graduate school at CCA my work began to change. I began to think more and more about barriers, how they functioned, and how to break them down. For me, the invisible barriers that we adhere to everyday— the rules through which we are socially conditioned—are much scarier that the physical ones we encounter while moving through the world. San Francisco is filled with cyclone fences topped with curled razor and barbed wire. I wanted to queer a fence and use craft to reconfigure the idea of a barrier. Furthermore, I wanted to use this barrier to queer predominant notions of craft. Around this time I also put down my knitting needles and began to knit on children's toy knitting machines, including a Barbie knitting machine from the 1970s. Using these toy 'knitting cranks', I churned out knitted cords and then hand-wove a 10-foot tall, 30-foot long, hot pink razor wire and cyclone fence.

When thinking about this piece I kept in mind the premise that all barriers are permeable. Additionally, I wanted to magnify the idea that most barriers serve multiple purposes. They both 'keep out' and contain, they can be aesthetically pleasing, intimidating, or a combination of the two, and have for centuries been built up, torn down, broken through and repaired over and over again. Walking through the city, I was struck by how the weave structure of cyclone fences mimicked the knitted stitch—single lines looped together over and over again. Knitting a cyclone fence set into motion a series of contradictions that operated like a row of dominoes, each one activating another.

below and opposite LACEY JANE ROBERTS, *Building It Up To Tear It Down*, 2009–2010.
Crank-knit yarn, hand-woven wire, steel poles, assorted hardware, 2.5 x 15 m.
Image courtesy the artist.

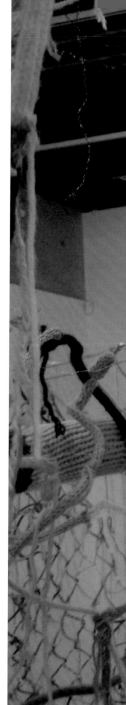

The hot pink colour and soft texture of the knitted fence is an automatic queering of the usual rigid steel used in typical cyclone fence construction. The pink yarn is neon and shocking, presenting a more in your face feminine touch rather than a soft one, and harks back to the pink used in militant queer movements and campaigns, such as the work produced by Gran Fury for ACT-UP. I then made further knit fences, in shiny steel grey that mimics the original chain link, only the yarn I used is filled with glitter, giving the piece a bejeweled

sparkle! In 2009–2010 I made a multicoloured version that was started using remnant yarn and evolved into a technicolour explosion.

The crank knitting machines used to stitch the yarn also require the use of the hand and occupy a space that is somewhere between the handmade and the industrial. The children's knitting machines put a magnified spin on a technique that was already considered amateur, cheap and feminine. The toy knitting machines require little skill to crank out long strands of stitches, and throw the mastery

often associated with fine craft into question. The fences are entirely hand woven—the knitted tubes threaded with a thin gauge wire and looped. Many of my pieces become a dare to myself. I challenge myself to construct an easily produced industrially manufactured object by hand as a test of endurance and patience. Additionally, this piece has been shown in a variety of contexts—several art galleries, a craft show, and outside on the street—in an attempt to show that one work can be categorised in many different areas, thus becoming unclassifiable.

PROGR

LOO

ESS: KING BACK

Curiously, the final section of this book has found itself looking backwards, rather than ahead, when searching for the future of knitting. Technical progress has unquestionably occurred —Freddie Robins' *Imperfect* series is one such example. But in equal measure are a number of projects that have come to recognise the remarkable feats of engineering, mathematics and design that informed the skills of hand knitting in the past. The machines that drive so much of our lives today are catching up, but they still have much to learn.

Sandy Black considers knitting as a hybrid practice, which she explains: "knitting has for me always been a combination of many things—textiles, fashion, craft, industry, design, art, technology and maths". Charting first the leaps and bounds that knitting has technically achieved in recent history, Black goes on to discuss the place of increasingly technical knitting in fashion and art.

Annie Shaw shares her recent research into the rich technical possibilities of hand production and finishing. Initially setting out to research machine knitting and technological innovation, Shaw found herself drawn back to the remarkable history of ganseys—fisherman's sweaters knit in the round by hand. Her own practice-led response to the gansey shows that looking to the past can sometimes be the best way to find the future.

Amy Twigger Holroyd provides an inspiring account of Keep & Share, her knitting business which has brought traditional values of customer care and long term satisfaction to the forefront of her modern business model. Like Shaw, Holroyd is interested in the potential of seamless production methods. But her sustainable business model engages as much with non-material sustainability strategies as it does the material. For example, Keep & Share has recently begun to hold knitting lessons at seemingly unlikely events such as literary and music festivals and invites the penny poor to suggest swaps of their services for garments.

Our final contributor, Rachel Beth Egenhoefer explains that her "Commodore 64 Computer and Fisher Price Loom are the defining objects of my childhood". Taking the technical as her starting point, Egenhoefer reminds us that computer code is basically a knitting pattern, a system of zeroes and ones that now runs our technology driven world. Egenhoefer's materials range from candy to resin, providing ways for us to see the immaterial code of computing rendered material and accessible.

In this final section, contributors reveal a future for knitting that may be as equally concerned with where it has come from as where it is going. The remarkable technical legacy of knitting makes the technical future of knitting as much about understanding and recovering the complexity of its past as it is imagining new futures. The importance of community to commerce, the unsurpassed technical feats of the past and an understanding of computing that dispels some of its off-putting complexity, all offer strategies for the future that I hope we will see deployed with increasing regularity in the decades to come.

KNITTING TECHNOLOGY COMES FULL CIRCLE

SANDY BLACK

Knitting is an intriguing hybrid: a practice which embraces both handcraft and industry, from everyday clothing and textiles to high fashion; a practice which has developed through hand skills, and inspired pioneering mechanical and electronic technology. Knitting is also a cultural phenomenon derived from an everyday domestic activity, which has over the course of history performed significant and socially useful functions in the community: from the patriotic knitting circles of wartime, to the fun and inclusive, semi-subversive, activities now familiar around the globe. 'Guerilla' knitting and knitting performances currently form one extreme of a spectrum, which spans art and craft, high fashion and commercial business. At the other, knitwear represents a multi-faceted, international industry spanning hosiery, knitted casual and outerwear, underwear, sports and leisurewear, and increasingly, high fashion for the international catwalks. In addition, there is a vast production of knitted jersey fabrics for fashion and everyday clothing, such as the ubiquitous t-shirt, and of warp knitted fabrics for interior, industrial and other technical uses, in, for example, automotive interiors and geotextiles. This diversity gives knitting its

fascination, but its commonplace and domestic context has meant it has often been overlooked in design and academic research contexts.

Knitting is both structure and form, a type of precision engineering, which is clearly demonstrated in applications that range from domestic handcraft to sophisticated industry. It can combine both two-dimensional fabric and three-dimensional form, a hybrid construction which can be fashioned to any shape, whilst simultaneously creating the textile structure it is made from. Extremes of scale and diverse materials constantly belie the structural similarities between types of knitted formation. The underlying constant in all of these is the knitted loop.

There are key commonalities between the hand knitted loop, those formed on the earliest knitting frames, and those using the most advanced contemporary industrial machines. Machine knitting, which pre-dated the Industrial Revolution by more than 150 years, originally emulated hand knitting. The precise method of loop forming, and the means of holding loops, has evolved and today it is one of the most sophisticated technologies. William Lee of Nottinghamshire first invented his mechanical knitting frame in 1589, and despite setbacks, technical improvements continued to be made, until by the end of the eighteenth century, production on the knitting frame had taken over all but the most remote cottage industry manufacture. However, the manual skills which created some of the virtuoso hand knitted and hand framed pieces of the eighteenth and nineteenth centuries have rarely been matched for fineness and intricacy, and certain mysteries remain: for example, what tools were used to construct the hand knitted masterpiece carpets of the Medieval guilds in Europe? Some of the earliest 'knitted' relics—known as Coptic socks—were not knitted on rods, but worked seamlessly in the round using the technique of single needle looping.[1] The felted caps ubiquitous in Medieval times were also knitted in the round without seams, and individually shaped by each maker according to requirements. More recently, the seamless revolution has, in the last 15 years, been heralded as the latest innovation in industrial knitting—but in fact it comes full circle, back to the techniques of the original hand knitters.

KNITTING AS CRAFT INDUSTRY

In Britain, hand knitting was an important industry, which thrived, particularly in Elizabethan times, in country regions and towns throughout England, Wales, Scotland and Ireland. Woollen cap knitting was one of the earliest industries, supported by many sumptuary laws during the fifteenth and sixteenth centuries, with much evidence of activity in centres such as Monmouth in Wales and the City of London, until the trade was gradually replaced by the fashionable demand for fine stockings.[2] Although there is no firm evidence, it is likely that coarse knitted stockings had been made for domestic use during the same period for women, children and labourers, but the invention of the stocking knitting frame by William Lee set in motion the industrialisation of the craft.[3] Knitting supplemented meagre incomes for numerous subsistence farming and fishing communities, and the hand knitting and machine knitting industries survived for a time side by side until hand knitting as an industry was ultimately replaced by mechanisation. Hand knitting became a leisure pursuit, but flourished again in times of need, during the wars of the nineteenth and twentieth centuries, and also when fashion rediscovered its delights. More recently, knitting as a metaphor for strong interconnections between people and things, is seen in contemporary artworks in response to an increasingly technological society in the twenty-first century.

In common with the early hand knitters and hand frame knitters of the sixteenth to nineteenth centuries, in the 1970s and 1980s it was still possible to base a knitting business on craft work and cottage industry production. The legacy of skills passed down over time through families, and through schooling in the needle arts, could still be found in ordinary people who knitted for both enjoyment and extra income. Many were housewives with childcare responsibilities, or people with disabilities, which kept them generally housebound.

These identities are in stark contrast to the early knitters who were peripatetic, with hands always occupied whilst tending flocks or walking to market. Several designer knitters, including myself, started businesses in the 1970s, making unique hand crafted knitwear for export markets around the world, using the skills of home knitters around the country. Added to this opportunity, was the fact that the industrial machinery of the time was not sophisticated enough to reproduce the intricate handwork created by the designer knitters. This fresh approach, particularly utilising colour mixing and pattern with complex structures, brought knitwear to the height of fashion once again. Since the turn of the new millennium, we have seen a revival and renewed appreciation of craft and the handmade, and the value of making things oneself, expressed through the medium of knitting.[4]

Although knitwear is not generally considered part of mainstream fashion—more a parallel production of staples and classics—knitwear cycles in and out of fashion with peaks of creative endeavour clearly influencing the fashion catwalks and seasonal calendar.[5] These cycles can often be linked to technological and social developments. In the last hundred years there have been several such peaks: in the 1920s and 1930s the new fibre rayon created waves in the textile industry, revolutionising the manufacture of hosiery and knitted fabrics; the 1940s and 1950s saw a burgeoning of smart tailored looks in imitation of rationed cloth tailoring, with a return to glamour after the hardships of war and knitting for victory, as was the case in the hand knitting craze of the 1920s; the 1970s saw the rise of more easy care synthetics and industrially made double jersey fabrics. As leisure activities have diversified and the pace of life quickened, hand knitting has had to speed up production to compete with mass manufactured items.

The British designer knitwear boom of the late 1970s and early 1980s was a direct reaction against mass produced fashions and classic knitwear, at a time when only a few pioneers of fashionable knitted dressing such as Missoni, Sonia Rykiel and Krizia existed. Knitwear then disappeared from fashion's view until key high fashion innovators such as Alaïa, Westwood, Gaultier, MacDonald and Yamamoto rediscovered the tactile, body enhancing and visually seductive qualities of knit. This interest came to a creative peak in the mid to late 1990s.[6] Since the 1970s and 1980s, the development of industrial knitting production has been influenced by the 'designer knitters' and by fashion designers who created new markets for style, shaping, pattern, colour imagery and surface structures. This period of fashion innovation coincided with, or possibly inspired, further technological developments in industrial knitting. Machines became capable of knitting complicated colour and structural patterns, including imitating popular hand knitting stitches such as Aran textures. Now technologically sophisticated knitwear production is available in every high street and designer store: intricately formed, unusually shaped or trimmed, perhaps deconstructed, wrapped, and fashioned in endless new ways to redefine fashion knitwear once more for the twenty-first century.

SANDY BLACK, *Lion & Unicorn*, 1984. Original Knits, wool sweaters.
Photograph by David McIntyre.

PERSPECTIVES ON KNITTING

On a personal level, knitting has for me always been a combination of many things—textiles, fashion, craft, industry, design, art, technology and maths. These diverse and often separated areas intersect and overlap within the design, construction and production of knitted artefacts; however, certain aspects prevail at different times and according to individual perspectives, needs and purposes. My own inspiration to develop a knitting business started when I was studying maths as an undergraduate student making rag-bag garments, drawing pictures on my graph paper, and collecting old knitting patterns and buttons.

Once I had bought my first domestic knitting machine, a cornucopia of possibilities for personal expression opened up through knitwear design. However, my early experiences confirmed knitting as a little understood hybrid of textiles and fashion, occupying the space between things: when I applied to the Crafts Council for support in the early years, I was turned down as too fashion oriented, whilst also being too craft-based for the fashion scene of the time. As part of a new wave of British fashion knitwear designers, knitting became my career: first as a self taught designer-maker; then as a designer and businesswoman running an international knitwear company, a publisher of knitting patterns and purveyor of Sandy Black yarns and knitting kits; finally I became an educator, author, researcher and commentator on knitting. My designs were made both on needles, and on domestic knitting machines using manual techniques, but I also worked with industrial manufacturing for clients, unusually spanning many types of production.

Several artists have recently adopted knitting to signal a repositioning of traditional women's work, and to provide an ironic and subversive humour, for example making hard masculine objects such as tanks and cars soft and feminine. The inherent perceptions of knit as old-fashioned, domestic and safe, which are embedded in the wider social consciousness, enable these works to succeed. The German artist Rosemarie Trockel, was one of the first to adopt industrial knitting as a metaphor and artist's medium. For Trockel, knitting became symbolic of the female, domestic and everyday, merging the commonplace and the political, exploiting the ability of knitting to be mass produced and manipulated in many ways.[7] Freddie Robins and Lisa Ann Auerbach have continued in this vein to subvert the familiar cosiness and normality of domestic machine knitting through their knitted artworks. Others, such as Germaine Koh take the activity of knitting itself as a performative practice or as a group social and political act.[8]

The emergence at the beginning of the new millennium of socially pro-active knitting groups in New York—Stitch 'n' Bitch by Debbie Stoller, and in London—Cast Off Knitting Club for Boys and Girls by Rachael Matthews and Amy Plant, sparked a massive popular following around the world. Do it yourself knitting groups sprung up everywhere, meeting in cafes, bars and all manner of public spaces. For these activist artists the act of creating knitted loops by hand is an inclusive approach, including a notable proportion of men at larger events. It is sufficient to generate new communities, supported by the phenomenal success of sharing experience via websites and blogs, which attract many tens of thousands of users.

Other artists and designers have taken a more material approach to the use of knitting as a commentary, working with the fabrication of loops in increasingly bizarre materials and structures. The knitted loop has fascinated artists who have embraced the immediacy and expressive nature of the craft through diverse materials—ceramic, carpet tape, or plastic bags for example. By manipulating extraordinary materials in an easily recognisable everyday knitted structure, an ironic statement is achieved. For example, Kelly Jenkins bent metal pipes into knitted formation for a functioning radiator, Susie MacMurray sculpted oversized loops into objects from carpet tape and manila rope, and Dave Cole knitted one of the heaviest materials, lead, into the shape and size of a grotesque child's teddy bear which would be impossible and dangerous to embrace.[9] Machiko Agano's and Shane Waltener's installations show us that the ethereal effect resulting from meshes of large-scale open knitting, or in Waltener's case fine webs, transcend the simplicity of the basic knitted loop structure to captivate or ensnare.

Precision can be seen in everything from the classic commercial 'fully fashioned' sweater to the mutated forms perfected in Freddie Robins' work. The fully fashioning techniques shape the knitting whilst it is being constructed, requiring precise calculations and movements of loops to narrow or widen the knitting and achieve the desired forms.[10] Robins' knitted artworks disturb and distort familiar realities and subvert knitwear construction. Body coverings are morphed into mutant garments, which themselves become the metaphor for the body, treading a disturbing line between the macabre and the humorous. Works such as *Headroom* become completely closed surfaces creating stifling and claustrophobic forms. Each piece is meticulously created in standard medium gauge plain knitted fabric on domestic knitting machinery with intricate shapings and features worked out with engineered exactitude, including facial features. Recently Robins has transferred her manual knitting machine approach to Shima Seiki industrial technology in order to render multiples, a kind of art mass production familiar from Damien Hirst's work; for example *Anyway*, an installation of multiple sweaters.[11] Mathematics is however fundamental to knitting, whether overtly calculated by the artist or knitter, or implicit in the knitting machine programming. A hidden artistry lies in the experience of the designer and technician and creative application of technological problem-solving to achieve a particular knitted aesthetic of perfection.

Many fashion designers traditionally approach knit as just another base material with greater properties of stretch and drape, but with little specific knowledge. Fashion designers have to rely on a team of specialists to realise their concepts in a two-way dialogue which pitches creative visions against technical feasibility. Knitwear design from first principles is a specialist activity which requires either personal knowledge of knitted structure or the interpretation of a skilled technician to transform a concept into a knitted reality. Whereas in the 1970s and 1980s the vision of designers could lead technological development forward, this position has been reversed since the mid 1990s, when a new wave of technical development in knitting machinery has left many designers with insufficient knowledge and unable to exploit this technology to the full.[12] In the hands of innovative designers, however, knit properties can be exploited to new ends. For example, in her winter 2002 collection Rei Kawakubo of Comme des Garçons utilised the stretch properties of knitted jersey fabrics to create totally distorted silhouettes in otherwise classic coats and jackets.

In contrast, other innovate techniques are the result of mechanical, rather than hand knitting developments. For example, warp knitting is a knitting technology that is not derived from hand knitting and cannot be reproduced by hand. It is a knitted structure formed from interlinking warp threads fed from a warp beam as in weaving. This construction is used for the APOC line by Issey Miyake and Dai Fujiwara, a truly revolutionary concept for seamless clothing, both technologically and aesthetically. APOC—named from the acronym A Piece Of Cloth—represents a paradigm shift in clothing concept. Instead of one piece of knitted cloth coming out of the machine, the clothing is liberated by cutting out, with no sewing or finishing processes required at all. A complete transformation takes place from two-dimensions to three-dimensions in one step via the opening out of a flat tubular construction, joined along sewing lines, similar to a woven fabric lay plan. Developed since 1999, APOC is an ongoing experiment in which mass production meets customisation. The roll of fabric, which comes off the knitting machine may contain a wardrobe of garments, whilst at the same time minimal waste and efficient production are both achieved.[13]

At the opposite extreme to the high technology of APOC, fashion collections in the first decade of the twenty-first century have also looked back to the comfortable and familiar handcrafted techniques of traditional knitting such as Fair Isle motifs, stripes and snowflakes. In tandem with the revival of social and leisure knitting, fashion has returned to the familiarity of oversized hand knitting on large needles. Fashion designers from Yohji Yamamoto and Giles Deacon to companies such as Byblos have used large-scale knits in recent collections, possibly inspired by the hand made creations of individuals such as Sandra Backlund and Simone Shailes, two recent design graduates whose experimental work has, aided by features in the press, been inordinately influential.

THE LOOP

Knitting is many things to many people—it can be cosy, sexy, decorative, classic, oversized, micro, clinging, enveloping, chunky, see-through, sophisticated or theatrical. But fundamental to all parts of the knitting spectrum is the structure of the knitted loop itself—the building block from which all knitted fabrics are derived. In fashion, the visible and hand knitted loop regularly appears and reappears in

cycles. As society returns to notions of hibernation and comfort, handcrafting prevails. On closer inspection, the barely visible loop provides the material for underwear, tights and stockings, t-shirts and even fleeces, as well as sweaters, socks, hats, gloves, scarves and cardigans. In addition to clothing and accessories, the most visible contemporary manifestation of knit looping is in the new knitting social groups who once again knit in public, presenting their creations online for all to see, together with a new generation of artists whose concern with both aesthetic and process fits the medium of knitting like the proverbial glove. The mass of metaphorical cultural baggage attached to knitting—the poverty, domesticity and femininity which still cling to its image—has now been harnessed by a new community who can begin to transcend preconceptions to subvert expectations. At the same time, the knitwear and hosiery industries are coming to terms with new global realities and harnessing the power of technology for innovation in technical areas. The fashion industry is broad enough to encompass all extremes of the loop, but paradoxically, as technology moves ahead in leaps and bounds, the familiar knitted loop of the hand knitter takes pride of place for impact.

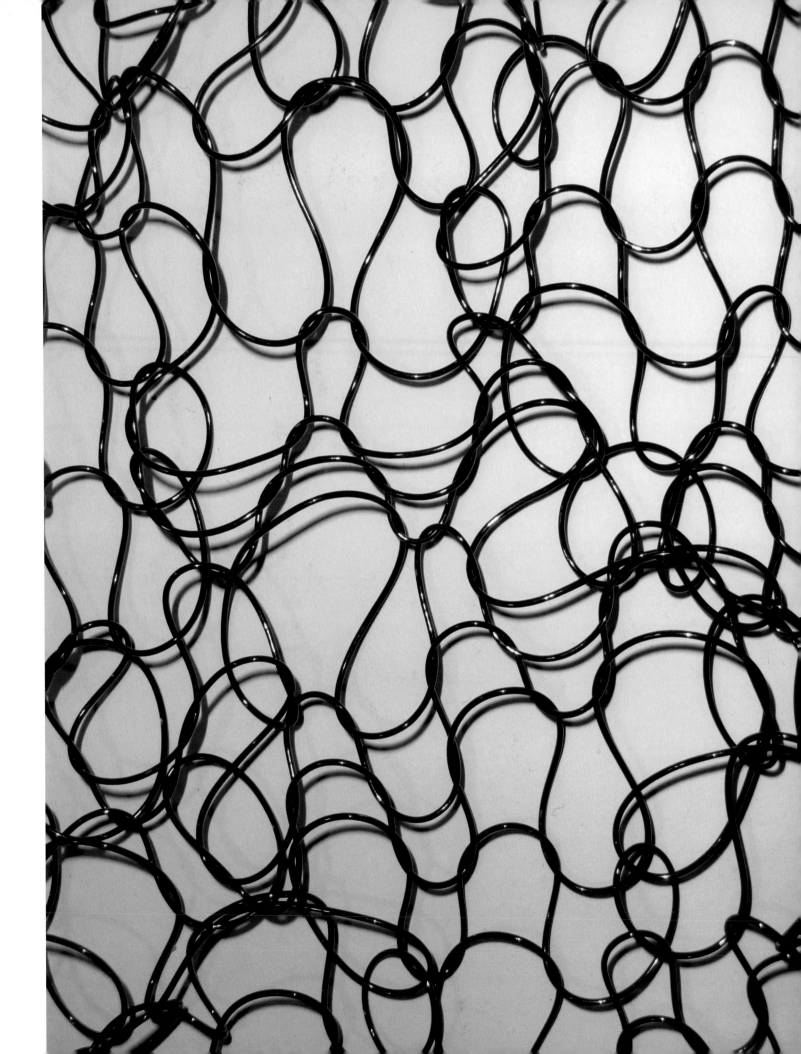

previous page SUZUMI NODA, randomly knitted plastic wire artwork, 2007.
Photograph by Sandy Black.
above SIMONE SHAILES, wool outfit from MA graduate collection, 2008.
Photograph by Chris Moore. Courtesy the designer.
opposite SANDY BLACK, *Tranquil Vale*, 1978. Original knits wool sweater.
Photograph by Barbara Bellingham. Image courtesy the designer.

LOOKING BACKWARDS TO LOOK FORWARDS

ANNIE SHAW

My practice uses a device of looking backwards to look forwards. Inspiration is drawn from the hand knitting of the fishing villages and ports of North-East Coastal Britain where most early hand knitted garments were made 'in the round' and seamlessly.

Although a knitting machine was invented as early as 1589, it was not until 1996 that a machine could produce a totally seamless outerwear garment. Using a multi-tubular technique and the associated SDS-One design system® the Shima Seiki SWG© technology produces knitted garments, which require no making up. The associated reduction in production costs signifies design opportunities for costs to be focused elsewhere, such as post-production.

The generic example of a gansey or fisherman's jumper was used as a basic form to develop new approaches to garment making. In a method which mirrors mass-customisation, 50 samples were knitted using WholeGarment® technology. Craft-like and 'situationist' techniques were then used to develop, subvert and interrogate mass-produced units. The ganseys were taken on an experimental, developmental

journey. Some of the experiments have commercial potential; others offer ideas that question the values of a globalised mass-produced fashion industry.

The experimental approach towards some of the ganseys could be described as crafting the technological. Craft-like techniques such as felting, printing and latex-dipping were used. Arbitrary mending and repair was incorporated. Chance finds from the tide-line and charity shops were used to embellish the designs.

In order to achieve post-production wearing and ageing and to make a direct narrative connection with location and the landscape I also explored sea-washing techniques. Ganseys were placed in a lobster creel at sea and removed after one, two and three months respectively. Largely unsubstantiated stories of drowned fishermen being identified by their ganseys persist to the present day. In these extreme experiments I worked to attach a romantic narrative to a garment to help reinforce emotional connection.

The Penny Hedge is an ancient tradition associated with Whitby Abbey. The Hedge is erected on Ascension Eve as an act of penance. It has to survive three tides and if it fails, land is forfeited to the Abbey. Seven ganseys were attached to the Penny Hedge and left for three tides. Three tides were not long enough to cause any great material damage to the garments, but this was never the real intention. The focus was on narrative and making a physical connection with location. I deep-fried a gansey at a Fish and Chip shop in Whitby to illustrate the connection between fast food and fast clothes. After the addition of salt and vinegar it was wrapped in newspaper and recorded photographically.

At a time when sustainability is a key design consideration, these post-knit processes give the garments 'slow' values, a sense of narrative and an emotional connection. It is hoped that this connection can help to make garments less disposable for both wearer and designer.

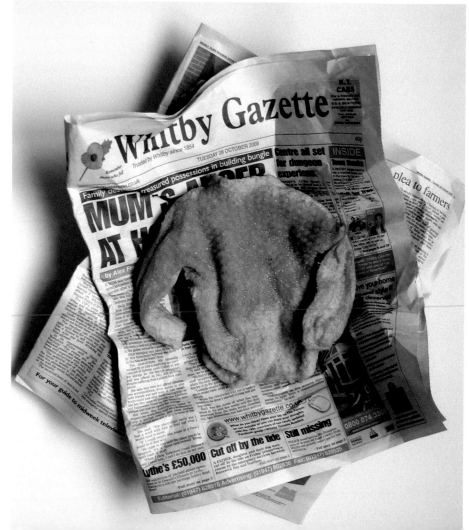

previous page ANNIE SHAW, 3-tide wash, Penny Hedge, Whitby. © Annie Shaw.
opposite top ANNIE SHAW, Lobster creel, sea-washed ganseys, Runswick Bay, North Yorkshire. © Annie Shaw.
opposite bottom ANNIE SHAW, Gansey, deep-fried at a fish and chip shop, Whitby, North Yorkshire. © Annie Shaw.
above ANNIE SHAW, Basic WholeGarment® seamlessly knitted ganseys. © Annie Shaw.

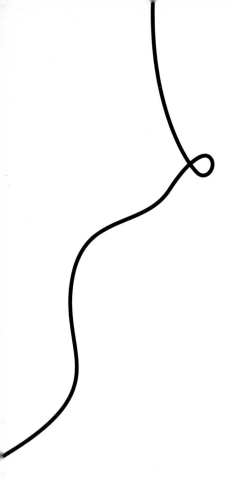

KEEP & SHARE

AMY TWIGGER HOLROYD

Keep & Share was conceived as an 'alternative luxury' knitwear label during my MA at Winchester School of Art in 2003. Having become interested in the potential of hi-tech seamless construction, I developed techniques for joining and gathering pieces seamlessly using domestic knitting machines.

Affronted by the huge quantities of clothing that we buy and discard each year, I was also interested in the sustainability concept of sufficiency, through an emphasis on longevity and versatility. My label strategy involves craft-scale manufacture and a combination of archetypal details with unconventional knit techniques.

Since launching the business in 2004, my experience has shown that the longevity I seek also depends on immaterial factors, such as the emotions of the customer towards their item and the relationship between designer and user.

Keep & Share provides a forum for exploring leftfield ideas: from loaning out pieces for a week, to hand-wash, repair and makeover services, and a new method of design in which I request inspirational 'snippets' from customers to form the basis of my collections.

The wish to create strong emotional ties between wearer and garment fostered the move, in 2008, to allow users to make their own pieces under the Keep & Share umbrella. Hand knitters can create Keep & Share designs from kits, while customers can also come to the studio to machine knit their own piece from start to finish in a single weekend.

Summer 2009 saw us take this message on the road, launching our knitting tent at literary and music festivals where we got hundreds of people knitting—whether learning for the first time or starting again after a long break. My underlying aim is to reintroduce people to the process of making, in a world where we are increasingly divorced from the production of the items we use and consume.

previous page AMY TWIGGER HOLROYD OF KEEP & SHARE, *Gladys Cardi*, 2008. UK-reared alpaca wool. Photograph by Meg Hodson.
opposite AMY TWIGGER HOLROYD OF KEEP & SHARE, *Dinky Cape Kit*, 2009.'Offcuts Yarn', a recycled yarn made from a mix of natural fibres. Image courtesy the artist.
above AMY TWIGGER HOLROYD OF KEEP & SHARE, *Bakersfield Jumper*, 2006. Wool, nickel buckle. Photograph by Meg Hodson.

opposite AMY TWIGGER HOLROYD OF KEEP & SHARE, *Eugenia Dress*, 2006. Cotton. Photograph by Meg Hodson.

top AMY TWIGGER HOLROYD OF KEEP & SHARE, *Gladys Cardi*, 2007. 100 per cent organic colour grown cotton. Photograph by Meg Hodson.

bottom AMY TWIGGER HOLROYD OF KEEP & SHARE, *Who Made This? Cardi*, 2009. Found cardigan. Photograph by Amy Twigger Holroyd.

above AMY TWIGGER HOLROYD OF KEEP & SHARE, Keep & Share Knitting Tent at Latitude Festival, 2009. Image courtesy the artist.
opposite top and bottom AMY TWIGGER HOLROYD OF KEEP & SHARE, Festival blanket (detail) with label, Green Man Festival, 2009. Image courtesy the artist.

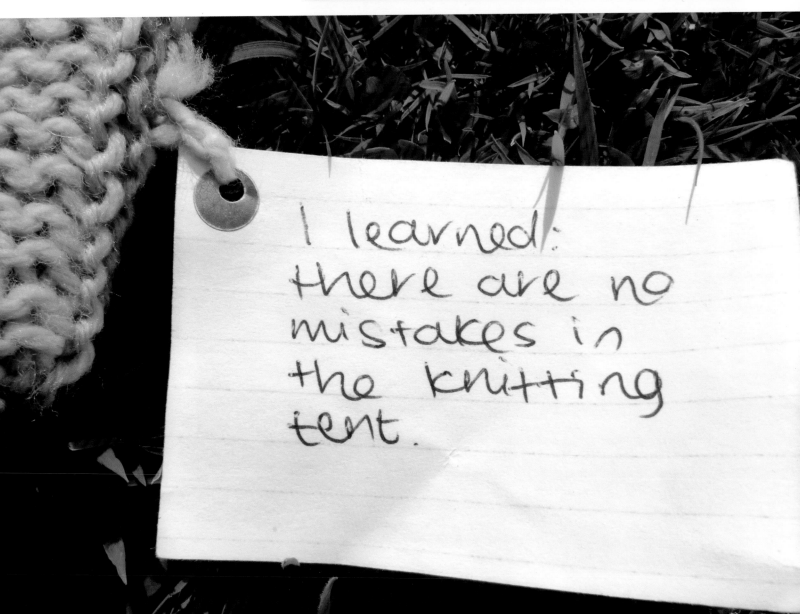

TRACKING KNITTING AND TRANSLATING CODE

RACHEL BETH EGENHOEFER

My work stems from an exploration of the connections between textiles and technology on historical, constructional, physical and conceptual levels. Textiles share historical connections to technology, its object oriented process serving as the blueprint for the immaterial processing of computing. They also share a constructional make-up that interests me more. Knitting, like computer code, is a base-two pattern: knits and purls, zeros and ones. Cloth provides the comfort and security of an object. It is tangible code we can see and understand, while giving us the same comfort as our own clothing accessorising our bodies.

Candy becomes an ideal medium to discuss that which is intangible, to represent that which does not physically exist in a form that evokes all of the senses. Able to not just see and touch sweets but also to hear, and smell, and of course taste, which can lead to desire. Candy in every state of its process is temporal. Fluctuating in the threshold of temperature candy reaches its ideal state to harden, only to change again, melting down with the atmospheric influences, and changing again with its desirable consumption. It exists as a tangible cyclical process.

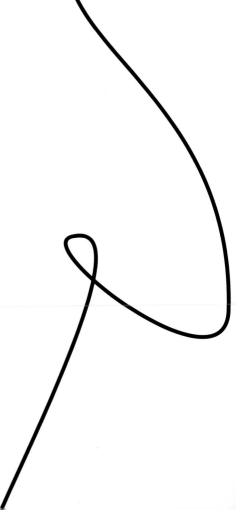

Tying together the processes and objects of my work is the circular looped motion that constructs our actions, desires, and movements. The cycles of analogue to digital information pulsating up and down a wave of electricity. The obvious cycles of the body's hunger and fulfilment intertwined with cycles of digestion. The motion of two hands knitting a string of yarn into cloth. The motion of our bodies interacting with machines, tensing and relaxing. Digital information plots points for electricity to flow through. Textile patterns plot the construction of cloth. While plotting points, like the grid, relationships become order, and order becomes connections.

I am interested in the intersection where all of these ideas can meet in artistic, critical, and rhetorical studies. I am interested in contemporary and historical issues in digital media, traditional craft, pop culture, and modern society. I do not consider my works to be solely 'digital media' or 'textile works', but rather are situated somewhere in-between. 'The space between' has been a place of interest not only for situating my work but also for exploration in my work. I find this meeting place a curious space for negotiation. As analogue information is being translated to digital, what happens in the space between the zero and the one? How

is the space between body and cloth formed on clothing? As our bodies interact with machines, what happens in the space between as we tense and relax, strain our muscles, and correct our bodies with ergonomic devices?

I work with both tangible and intangible materials, twisting, looping, pressing, attaching, inserting, assembling. My hands become input devices to transform ideas through materials into works. Just as the keyboard and mouse are input devices for the computer, knitting needles become input devices for yarn to be cast into cloth. If knits and purls can be interchanged for zeros and ones, I ask if the input devices could be interchanged as well.

My work explores the intersection of technology and textiles. Knits and purls of patterns are strung together just as zeros and ones create code. One is tactile and material; the other completely intangible. I am interested in how our bodies interact with machines and with cloth, both consciously and subconsciously, and what exists in the space between. I loop the yarn to knit while my hands create circles with needles. Sitting at the keyboard my shoulders tense and relax in cycles of work, while infinite algorithms run looped programmes on my computer. Silly, isn't it, to knit intangible objects that fit the space between?

previous page RACHEL BETH EGENHOEFER, *Knit Negotiation*, 2004. Sweater for the space between you and your machine. I was thinking about the ergonomic wrist supports and other devices that we wear in order to make computers and machines safer for us to use. I found it odd that we are the ones having to put things on. This sweater was designed so both you and the computer have to put something on in order to be comfortable.

left and right RACHEL BETH EGENHOEFER, *Untitled (lollipop grid)*, 2004–2005. Lollipops in wall, dimensions variable. Lollipops are installed directly into the wall, 15 cm apart from one another in a floor to ceiling grid. Dimensions variable depending on space. While making obvious connections to order and structure, the candy grid also references children's board games and evokes a sense of play; asking the viewer to establish rules of order, play, and desire. The polka dotted grip creates an optical illusion, appearing flat when viewed from a distance, and changes perceptive as you move in relation to the piece and the cast shadows. The physical qualities of candy evoke the senses allowing viewers to see, smell, and desire to taste the piece as the fragrant sugar aromatises the space. The temporal aspects of candy cause the lollipops to slowly change shape, drip, create puddles, and eventually dissolve.

opposite RACHEL BETH EGENHOEFER, *Yarn*, 2008. Knit ethernet cable, 35 x 30 x 30 cm. Image courtesy the artist.

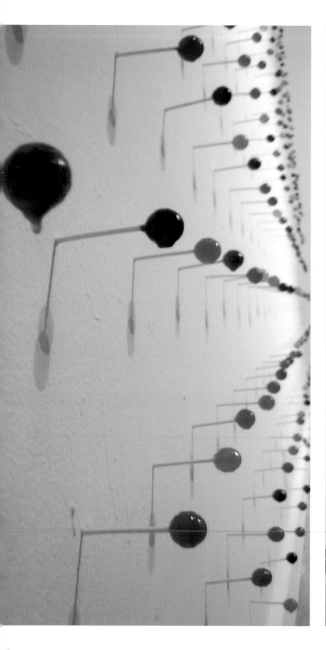

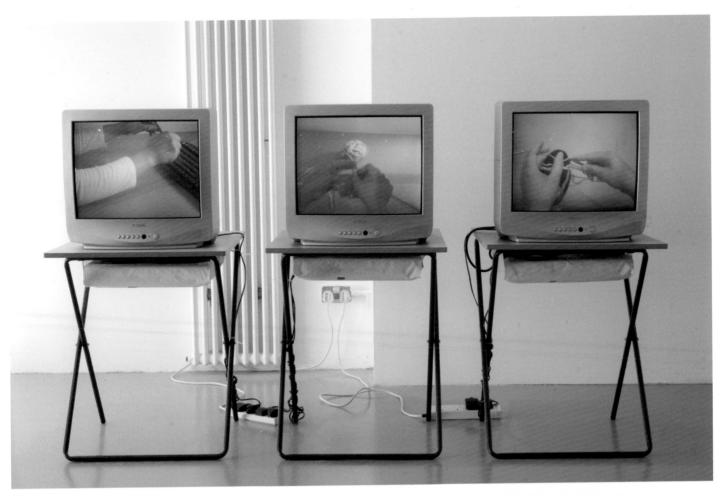

opposite RACHEL BETH EGENHOEFER, *Looped*, 2008. Steel zoetrope and knit animation, 25.5 cm tall x 48 cm diameter. Zoetrope showing the motion of two hands knitting. The inner strip of animated drawings is made of cloth constructed on a computerised knitting machine where each pixel becomes a stitch. When spun and viewed through the slits, viewers see the circular movement of hands looping knit stitches. Viewers encouraged to spin.

top RACHEL BETH EGENHOEFER, *Input*, 2008. Three channel video. Non-linear video of fingers inputting information in a keyboard, then replaced by knitting needles as the mouse becomes a tool for knitting, and the hands intertwine between.

bottom RACHEL BETH EGENHOEFER, *Virtual Knitting, in progress, knitting in physical and virtual space*, 2008. Knit cloth is tangibly constructed from series of knit and purl stitches. Code is constructed from intangible sets of zeros and ones. Here users are able to knit in both physical and virtual space at the same time, constructing both tangible and intangible cloth. The motion of interacting with the knitting needles as an input device for the computer references other of my works that relate to human/machine interaction.

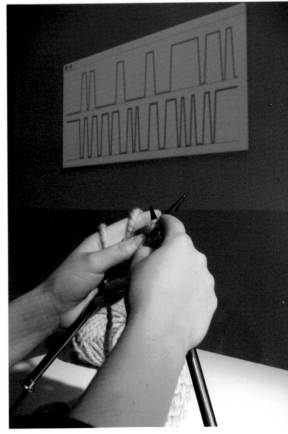

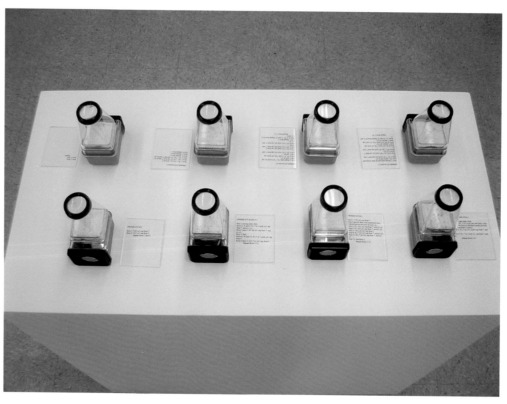

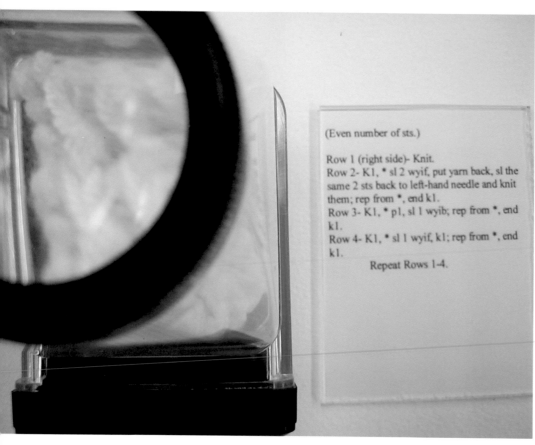

(Even number of sts.)

Row 1 (right side)- Knit.
Row 2- K1, * sl 2 wyif, put yarn back, sl the same 2 sts back to left-hand needle and knit them; rep from *, end k1.
Row 3- K1, * p1, sl 1 wyib; rep from *, end k1.
Row 4- K1, * sl 1 wyif, k1; rep from *, end k1.

Repeat Rows 1-4.

opposite and below RACHEL BETH EGENHOEFER, *Variations on a Theme*, 2003. Two-way viewers, knitting, code, 5 x 15 x 7.5 cm, series of eight different patterns. Eight different 2.5 cm samples of knitting patterns are displayed in two-way magnified viewers. Next to each viewer the 'code' is displayed in the simplest terms, drawing parallels between knitting patterns and computer codes. Image courtesy the artist.

opposite and below RACHEL BETH EGENHOEFER, *KNiiTTiiNG®*, 2008–2009. Knitting for the Nintendo Wii, created in collaboration with Kyle E Jennings, © www.KNiiTTiiNG.com. The motion and actions of knitting are converted into interactions with the Nintendo Wii. Rather than being generic movements however, users need to actually decipher the differences between the motions of knitting and the motions of purling, wrapping the yarn, and transferring stitches. While still in early beta stages, the end goal is modelled after games such as *Dance Dance Revolution* or *Guitar Hero*, users are challenged to follow knits and purls on screen moving in rhythm with the game, and without dropping a stitch! In *KNiiTTiiNG* however, players can only knit a 'virtual cloth', as apposed to performing a dance or singing a song, which relates to other of my works that reference tactility and code, while also bringing in elements of pop culture and scatological video games.

AFTERWO

END NOTES

TWISTS, KNOTS & HOLES: COLLECTING, THE GAZE & KNITTING THE IMPOSSIBLE

1. Stewart, Susan, *On Longing*, Durham and London: Duke University Press, 1993, p. 162.
2. Stewart, *On Longing*, p. 162.
3. Lacan, Jacques, "Out of the Blue", *Time and the Image*, Parveen Adams trans., Manchester: Manchester University Press, 2000, p. 61.
4. McGowan, Todd, *The Real Gaze: Film Theory After Lacan*, Albany: State University of New York Press, 2007, p. 6.
5. Lacan maintains the Freudian distinction between drive and instinct. For Lacan, where "instinct" denotes a pre-linguistic need, 'the drive is completely removed from the realm of biology. The drives differ from biology in that they can never be satisfied, and do not aim at an object but rather circle perpetually round it. The purpose of the drive is not to reach a goal but to return to its circular path and to elicit enjoyment through the repetitive movement of the closed circuit'. Dylan Evans, *An Introductory Dictionary of Lacanian Psychoanalysis*, London: Routledge, 1996, pp. 46–47.
6. McGowan, *The Real Gaze: Film Theory After Lacan*, p. 28.
7. Crone, Rainer and Petrus G Schaesberg, *Louise Bourgeois: The Secret of the Cells*, Munich, London, New York: Prestel, p. 104.
8. We are indebted here to the exegisis of the different properties of the staged fantasy scene, McGowan, *The Real Gaze: Film Theory After Lacan*, 2007.

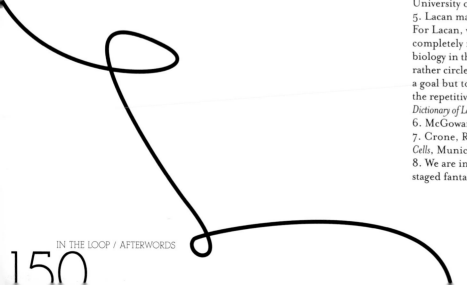

'THE FLOW OF ACTION': KNITTING, MAKING AND THINKING

1. An important knitting scholar as well as a practitioner, Richard Rutt published *A History of Hand Knitting* in 1987. Montse Stanley designed, researched and published about knitting history and practice. She was a founder of The Early Knitting History Group and co-curated a landmark exhibition on knitting for the Textile Museum, Terrassa, Spain.

2. Rutt, *A History of Hand Knitting*, pp. 116–117.

3. Ingold, Tim, "Tool-use, Sociality and Intelligence", *Tools, Language and Cognition in Human Evolution*, K R Gibson and Tim Ingold eds, Cambridge: Cambridge University Press, 1993, p. 419.

4. Ingold, Tim, "Situating Action V. The History and Evolution of Bodily Skills", *Ecological Psychology*, vol. 8, no. 2, 1997, p. 179.

5. Gibson, K R, "General Introduction. Animal Minds, Human Minds", *Tools, Language and Cognition*, p. 9.

6. Rutt, *A History of Hand Knitting*, p. 137.

7. See, for example, Sharon Kirchoff, *Memories: How I learned to Knit*. http://www.helium.com/items/806818-memories-how-i-learned-to-knit, accessed 28 June 2008.

8. Ingold, "Situating Action V," p. 179.

9. Matthews, Steven G, "The Instantiated Identity: Critical Approaches to Studying Gesture and Material Culture." Essay presented at the Materialisation of Social Identities session, annual Theoretical Archaeology Group conference, University of Glasgow, Scotland, 17–19 December 2004. http://www.semioticon.com/virtuals/archaeology/instantiated.pdf, accessed 20 June 2008.

10. See Carter's 1880 watercolour *The Knitting Lesson*. For image, see http://habetrot.typepad.com/habetrot/2007/02/index.html; for sale details, see http://www.artnet.com/Artists/LotDetailPage.aspx?lot_id=69C3DA64377930B09CC6D997051EAF6A, accessed 2 July 2008. George, Jacqueline, *Your Stories of Learning to Knit*, Victoria & Albert Museum. http://www.vam.ac.uk/collections/fashion/features/knitting/your_stories/index.php, accessed 28 November 2008.

11. Fleetwood, Katie, "Knitting… Frumpfest or the New Rock'n'Roll?", unpublished essay, Textile Conservation Centre, 2007.

12. Elizabeth Zimmermann presented a popular American television series on knitting. Her books include *Knitting without Tears*, 1971, and *The Knitter's Almanac*, 1981.

13. Ingold, "Situating Action V. The History and Evolution of Bodily Skills", pp. 178–179.

14. Mauss, Marcel, "Techniques of the Body", *Economy and Society*, vol. 2, p. 79. It should be noted that Ingold critiques the Maussian model.

15. Ingold, "Situating Action V. The History and Evolution of Bodily Skills", p. 179.

16. Rutt, *A History of Hand Knitting*, pp. 121–122.

17. Rutt, *A History of Hand Knitting*, p. 17, pp. 20–21.

18. Rutt, *A History of Hand Knitting*, p. 17, pp. 125–126.

19. Matthews, Steven G, "The Materiality of Gesture: Intimacy, Emotion and Technique in the Archaeological Study of Bodily Communication." Essay presented at The Archaeology of Gesture: Reconstructing Prehistoric Technical and Symbolic Behaviour, 11th Annual Meeting of the Association of Archaeologists, Cork, Ireland, 5–11 September 2005. http://www.semioticon.com/virtuals/archaeology/materiality.pdf, accessed 20 June 2008.

20. Frost, Annie S, *Ladies' Guide to Needlework*, 1877, cited in Richard Rutt, *A History of Hand Knitting*, p. 18.

21. Rutt, *A History of Hand Knitting*, pp. 17–18.

22. Ibsen, Henrik, *The Doll's House*, 1879, Act III. http://www.gutenberg.org/dirs/etext01/dlshs11.txt, accessed 15 June 2008.

23. Thomas, Mary, "Our Knitting Forces", *The Queen's Book of the Red Cross*, London: Hoddder & Stoughton, 1939.

24. Booth, Cherie and Cate, Hate, *The Goldfish Bowl. Married to the Prime Minister 1955–1997*, London: Chatto & Windus, 2004, p. 75.

25. Dunn, J, *Antonia White: A Life*, London: Virago Press, 2000, p. 43.

26. Sayers, Dorothy L and Jill Paton, Walsh, *Thrones, Domination*, London: Hodder & Stoughton, 1998, pp. 39–40. Sayers' unfinished novel was completed by Walsh.

SPINNING STRAW INTO GOLD: THE 'NEW' WOMAN IN CONTEMPORARY KNIT LIT

1. LaZebnik, Claire, *Knitting Under the Influence*, New York: 5 Spot Publishing, 2006, cover.

2. Vicinus, Martha, *Suffer and be Still*, Indianapolis: Indiana University Press, 1973.

3. Radway, Janice, *Reading the Romance: Women, Patriarchy and Popular Literature*, London: Verso, 1987, p. 61.

4. "She held up the oft-neglected circular sweater and examined the rose-coloured yarn. Row after row of neat stockinette stitches She was going to finish this sweater at last" Sefton, Maggie, *A Deadly Yarn*, New York: Berkley Prime Crime, 2006, p. 257.

5. Sefton, *A Deadly Yarn*, p. 32.

6. Ferris, Monica, *Crewel World*, New York: Berkley Publishing, 1999, p. 47.

7. Kruger, Mary, *Died in the Wool*, Boston: Pocket Books, 2005, p. 1.

8. Kruger, Mary, *Knit Fast Die Young*, Boston: Pocket Books, 2007.

9. Kruger, *Died in the Wool*, back cover.

10. Mizejewski, Linda, *Hardboiled and High Heeled: The Woman Detective in Popular Culture*, London and New York: Routledge, 2004, p. 23.

11. Radway, *Reading the Romance*, p. 149.

12. Wolf, Naomi, *Promiscuities: A Secret History of Female Desire*, London: Vintage, 1998, pp. 67–94.

13. The term, and 'chick lit', refers to a genre of novels aimed at and written by women, emerging as a response to Helen Fielding's *Bridget Jones's Diary*, 1996. Walter, Natasha, *The New Feminism*, London: Virago, 1999, pp. 186–187.

14. Discussion with Marian Keyes, Kelly Gyenes "Chick lit: Sex, shoes.... And substance", CNN, 8 September 2006, see http://www.cnn.com/2006/SHOWBIZ/books/09/07/chick.lit/index.html and Gina Frangello, "Is Chick Lit the Culprit?", 29 April 2006, see http://ginafrangello.blogs.com/gina_frangello/2006/04/is_chick_lit_th.html

15. Examples include John Gray, *Men are from Mars Women are From Venus*, London & New York: Harper Collins, 1992.

16. Lazebnik, *Knitting under the Influence*, p. 59.

17. McNeil, Gill, *Divas Don't Knit*, London: Bloomsbury, 2007, p. 117.

18. Goldsmith, Olivia, *Wish Upon a Star*, London and New York: Harper Collins, 2004, pp. 201–202.

19. "The Craft Yarn Council reports that in 2002, 13 percent of women ages 25–34 knitted; by 2004, that figure had more than doubled to 33 percent", Natalie Danford, "The End of the Yarn?", *Publishers Weekly*, 28 August 2006.

20. Mulvey, Laura, "Visual Pleasure and Narrative Cinema", *The Sexual Subject: A Screen Reader in Sexuality*, London: Routledge, 1992, pp. 22–34.

21. Levy, Ariel, *Female Chauvinist Pigs: Women and the Rise of Raunch Culture*, London: Pocket Books, 2006, p. 172.

22. Benjamin, Walter, referenced in Sue Rowley, "There Once Lived.... Craft and Narrative Traditions" in Sue Rowley, ed., *Craft and Contemporary Theory*, St Leonards: Allen and Unwin, 1997. Rowbotham, Sheila, *Hidden from History: 300 Years of Women's Oppression and the Fight Against It*, London: Pluto Press, 1977.

KNITTING IN SOUTHERN AFRICAN FICTION

1. LaDuke, Betty, *Africa: Women's Art, Women's Lives*, Trenton, New Jersey; Asmara, Eritrea: Africa World Press Inc., 1997, p. 117.

2. Jay, Floss M, "Knitting Gloves", *LIP From Southern African Women*, Susan Brown, Isabel Hofmeyer & Susan Rosenberg, eds, Johannesburg: Raven Press, 1983, p. 33.

3–12. Jay, *LIP From Southern African Women*, p. 33.

13. Jay, *LIP From Southern African Women*, p. 34.

14–18. Jay, *LIP From Southern African Women*, p. 35.

19–21. Jay, *LIP From Southern African Women*, p. 36.

22. Chikwave, Brian, *Harare North*, London: Jonathan Cape, 2009, pp. 6–7.

23–24. Chikwave, *Harare North*, p. 7.

25–26. Chikwave, *Harare North*, p. 14.

27–30. Chikwave, *Harare North*, p. 15.

31–32. Chikwave, *Harare North*, p. 16.

33. Dangarembga, Tsitsi, *The Book of Not*, Banbury: Ayebia Clarke Publishing, 2006, p. 3.

34. Dangarembga, *The Book of Not*, p. 7.

35. Dangarembga, *The Book of Not*, p. 129.

36. Dangarembga, *The Book of Not*, p. 130.

37. Dangarembga, *The Book of Not*, p. 132.

38. Dangarembga, *The Book of Not*, p. 136.

39. Dangarembga, *The Book of Not*, p. 137.

40. Dangarembga, *The Book of Not*, p. 138.

41. Dangarembga, *The Book of Not*, p. 129.

TEXTILES AND ACTIVISM

1. Maharaj, Sarat, "Arachne's Genre: Towards Inter-Cultural Studies in Textiles," *Material Matters: The Art and Culture of Contemporary Textiles*, Ingrid Bachmann & Ruth Scheuing, eds, Toronto: YYZ Books, Canada 1998, pp. 157–196.

2. All student quotes, unless otherwise noted, come from anonymous feedback questionnaires that were handed out at the end of the class. All are quoted with permission.

3. Course readings were drawn from a coursepack, in combination with selections from Livingstone, Joan and John Ploof, eds, *The Object of Labor: Art, Cloth and Cultural Production*, Chicago and Cambridge: University of Chicago Press and MIT Press, 2007.

4. Hickey, Georgina and Peggy C Hargis, "Teaching Eighties Babies Sixties Sensibilities", *Radical History Review*, vol. 84, Fall 2002, pp. 149–165.

5. It is, in fact, often at the moments of greatest frustration when I am surprised by students and am forced to look back at myself and my own assumptions.

6. The Revolutionary Knitting Circle, http://knitting.activist.ca/ *The Revolutionary Knitting Circle Proclamation of Constructive Revolution*.

7. Rinehart, Jane A, "Collaborative Learning, Subversive Teaching, and Activism," *Teaching Feminist Activism: Strategies from the Field*, Nancy A Naples and Karen Bojar, eds, New York and London: Routledge, 2002, pp. 22–35.

8. Rinehart, *Teaching Feminist Activism: Strategies from the Field*, p. 24.

9. Robbins, Bruce, "The Sweatshop Sublime," *PMLA: Publications of the Modern Language Association of America*, vol. 1, iss. 1, January 2002, pp. 84–98.

10. Shenk, Gerald and David Takacs, "Using History to Inform Political Participation in a California History Course," *Radical History Review*, vol. 84, Fall 2002, pp. 138–148.

11. Shenk and Takacs, *Radical History Review*, p. 140.

ENCOUNTERING 'THE BOGEY': THE SEPARATE—BUT—PARALLEL (AND NON-MERCENARY) CULTS OF CRAFTIVISM AND UNSENTIMENTAL WANTON SEXUALITY, POST-2001

1. Berens, Jessica and Kerri Sharp, eds, *Inappropriate Behaviour*, London: Serpent's Tail, 2002, p. 3, http://www.urban75.com/Mag/prada.html, accessed 20 January 2010.

2. In 2009 I published several scholarly blogs for *The Online Journal of Modern Craft: Academic Research on Craft* by Berg Publishers, London, Kevin Murray, ed., http://journalofmoderncraft.com/. The first part of this essay is directly from the beginning of my blog, posted on 10 November 2009, entitled "Performing Civic Craftivism" at http://journalofmoderncraft.com/category/responses/page/2.

3. *The Sexual Life of Catherine M.* was published in France, 2001, and England, 2002, sparking worldwide debate. The author of the candid memoire is an intellectual and, as such, has been the founder and editor of *Art Press* arts magazine, circulation 30,000, launched approximately 1970.

4. With acknowledgement to the 'masked prankster' who defeats 'smug complacency' and starts an 'orgy-cum-uprising'! Berens, Jessica and Kerri Sharp, eds, *Inappropriate Behaviour*, London: Serpent's Tail, 2002, p. 6, http://www.urban75.com/Mag/prada.html, accessed 20 January 2010.

5. I have referenced Jessica Beren's interview of Catherine Millet, entitled "The Double Life of Catherine M.", *The Guardian*, UK, http://www.guardian.co.uk/books/2002/may/19/biography.features, accessed 10 January 2010.

6. Direct quote from above article. Beren states that Catherine Millet does not do this.

7. Sex blog examples include *Girl with a One-Track Mind*—http://girlwithaonetrackmind.blogspot.com/—author: Abbey Lee, pen name of Zoe Margolis; *Belle de Jour*—http://belledejour-uk.blogspot.com/—author: Brooke Magnanti; and *Bitchy Jones's Diary*—http://bitchyjones.wordpress.com/all-about-bitchy/.

8–9. Warner, Marina, *No Go The Bogeyman: Scaring, Lulling and Making Mock*, London: Vintage, 2000, p. 3.

10. See new theoretical information on the history and philosophy of kindness, currently undergoing re-analysis such as the book *On Kindness* by Adam Phillips and Barbara Taylor, Hamish Hamilton, 2009.

11. My interpretation of Catherine Millet from two interviews: "The Art of Being on Display" by Margaret Simons in *The Age*, 24 May 2003, http://www.theage.com.au/articles/2003/05/23/1053585702176.html, accessed 10 January 2010, and the statement "She is married to Jacques Henric, an avant-garde poet and novelist, and has been monogamous for eight years" by Jessica Berens in "The Double Life of Catherine M.", *The Guardian*, UK, http://www.guardian.co.uk/books/2002/may/19/biography.features, accessed 10 January 2010.

KNITTING TECHNOLOGY COMES FULL CIRCLE

1. Burnham, Dorothy, "Coptic Knitting: an ancient technique", *Textile History*, vol. 3, 1972, pp. 116–124.

2. Buckland, Kirstie, "The Monmouth Cap", *Costume*, vol. 13, 1979, pp. 23–37; and "A Sign of Some Degree—the Mystery of Capping", *Text: for the study of Textile Art, Design and History*, vol. 36, 2008, pp. 40–45.

3. Hartley, Marie and Ingilby, Joan, *The Old Hand Knitters of the Dales*, second edition, Otley, Yorkshire: Smith Settle, 2001, [1951], p. 6; Farrell, Jeremy, *Socks and Stockings*, London: Batsford, 1992.

4. A raft of 'new wave' books on knitting and crafting have appeared since 2003, mirroring the previous boom in knit publications in the mid 1980s, e.g. Stoller, Debbie, *Stitch 'n' Bitch* series; *Making Stuff: An Alternative Craft Book*, London: Black Dog Publishing; Gschwandtner, Sabrina, *Knit Knit*, and many others on customising t-shirts etc..

5. For a full account see Black, Sandy, *Knitwear in Fashion*, London: Thames & Hudson, 2002.

6. Black, *Knitwear in Fashion*.

7. Black, *Knitwear in Fashion*, pp. 132–143.

8. See *Selvedge*, 9 Feb 2006, p. 88, for a review by Sandy Black of Koh's lifelong artwork *Knitwork* performed in Angel Row Gallery Nottingham, 2005.

9. Part of her Royal College of Art London MA graduate show, 2004. Part of her graduate show, 2004, and shown in the Knit 2 Together exhibition, Crafts Council, 2005. Dave Cole, *Knit Lead Teddy Bear*, 2006, *Radical Lace and Subversive Knitting*, exhibition catalogue, New York: Museum of Arts and Design, 2007.

10. Black, *Knitwear in Fashion*, pp. 132–135.

11. Wood, Katharine, ed., *Cosy*, exhibition catalogue of Freddie Robins' work, Colchester: Firstsite Gallery, 2002.

12. Black, Sandy, "Innovative Knitwear using seamless and unconventional construction", Proceedings of International Federation of Fashion Technology Institutes (IFFTI), 5th Annual Conference. Hong Kong, November 2002; Sayer, Kate N, Simon Challis, and Jacqueline A Wilson, "Seamless knitwear—the design skills gap", *The Design Journal*, vol. 10, no. 1, 2007.

13. Black, *Knitwear in Fashion*, pp. 118–123.

PAUL WHITTAKER is Senior Lecturer and Director of Education at the University of Southampton, Winchester School of Art. He has exhibited nationally and internationally, led research seminars on European identity and difference at the University of Massachusetts and published conference papers for the Higher Education Academy. His research interests centre on promoting innovation through the reconsideration of established practices by way of unconventional means, and experimentation and speculation regarding temporality and time in the creative process.

CLIO PADOVANI is a graduate of Edinburgh College of Art and the Royal College of Art. After training in tapestry and establishing a track record exhibiting internationally, she began researching the conceptual and technical time-based similarities between woven and moving images. In 2000, her first video and tapestry piece *Own Time* was acquired by the Crafts Council as the first moving image work in the Textile Collection. In 2002, she was short listed for the Jerwood Applied Arts Prize: Textiles and received a nomination for The Arts Foundation Textile Art shortlist, 2010.

FREDDIE ROBINS is an artist based in Essex. She uses knitting to explore contemporary issues such as gender, the domestic and the human condition. Her studio practice questions conformity and notions of normality and challenges the categories of art and craft. Recent exhibitions include Radical Lace & Subversive Knitting at the Museum of Arts & Design in New York; Skill, a Think Tank exhibition touring Europe; Dress Codes: Clothing as Metaphor at Katonah Museum of Art in New York; and The Art of Fashion: Installing Allusions at Boijmans van Beuningen Museum in The Netherlands. Her work is held in public collections including the Victoria and Albert Museum, Crafts Council and The West Norway Museum of Decorative Art in Bergen. She is Senior Tutor in Mixed Media at the Royal College of Art in London. www.freddierobins.com

SABRINA GSCHWANDTNER is a New York City based visual artist and writer. Her artwork has been exhibited internationally at venues such as the Museum of Arts & Design, New York; the Fleming Museum, Vermont; Contemporary Arts Centre, Lithuania; Gustavsbergs Konsthall, Sweden; the Contemporary Jewish Museum in San Francisco; and the Brooklyn Academy of Music. She is the recipient of an International Artists Studio Program in Sweden (IASPIS) grant and two MacDowell Colony fellowships. Her book *KnitKnit: Profiles and Projects from Knitting's New Wave* was published by Stewart, Tabori & Chang in 2007. From 2002–2007 she edited and published the art journal *KnitKnit*, which is now in the permanent collections of The Museum of Modern Art, New York, and the Fogg Art Museum at Harvard University. She earned a BA in art/semiotics from Brown University and an MFA from Bard College. http://www.knitknit.net

LINDA NEWINGTON studied for a BA Fine Art, Painting and graduated with a first class honours degree from Winchester School of Art. She then moved to London and worked as a Library Assistant at the British Museum: Natural History, in the Botany Library curating the collection of botanical drawings, paintings and prints. During this time she trained as a librarian and is now the Faculty Leader for Law, Arts and Social Sciences at the University of Southampton Library. In 2007 she completed an MA in the History of Textiles and Dress, with the Textile Conservation Centre. Her dissertation focused on the image and status of knitting in relation to the Knitting Collections held by the University Library. She has responsibility for special collections, which include the Artists' Books Collection and the Knitting Reference Library. In 2008, she co-organised, with Jessica Hemmings, the conference In the Loop: Knitting Past, Present and Future.

MARY M BROOKS read English at Cambridge University and subsequently worked in publishing and then in management consultancy. Having decided to develop her long-term interest in textiles, she took the Postgraduate Diploma in Textile Conservation at the Textile Conservation Centre, then at Hampton Court Palace. Mary returned to the Textile Conservation Centre in 1998 as Head of Studies & Research. At the University of Southampton, she became Reader and was Programme Leader for the MA Museums & Galleries. In 2002, Mary was a Conservation Scholar at the Getty Conservation Institute, Los Angeles, where she undertook research into regenerated protein fibres. She now runs her own consultancy focusing on objects, projects and people in conservation and museums. www.marymbrooks.co.uk

JO TURNEY is the course leader of MA Investigating Fashion Design at Bath Spa University. She gained her PhD from the University of Southampton in 2003, in which she investigated the cultural significance of amateur needlecrafts in Britain from 1970-2002. She is the co-author with Rosemary Harden of *Floral Frocks*, Antique Collectors Club, 2007 and author of *The Culture of Knitting*, Berg, 2009.

RAPHIES

Her main research interests include everyday textiles and dress, crafts criticism and critical theory. She is currently researching the relationship between dress and deviant behaviour, and a book about 1970s fashion.

MARK NEWPORT is an artist and educator living in Bloomfield Hills, Michigan. Newport's work has been exhibited throughout the United States, Canada, and Europe, including solo exhibitions at The Arizona State University Art Museum, The Cranbrook Art Museum, The Chicago Cultural Center, and here gallery, Bristol, England. His work is included in the collections of The Whitney Museum of American Art, The Cranbrook Art Museum, The Racine Art Museum, 4Culture in Seattle, City of Phoenix Public Art, Microsoft, and Progressive Insurance. Newport is the Artist-in-Residence and Head of Fiber at the Cranbrook Academy of Art. He earned his BFA from the Kansas City Art Institute in 1986 and his MFA from the School of the Art Institute of Chicago in 1991. www.marknewportartist.com

JEANETTE SENDLER studied costume design, MDes in Theatre Costume, at Edinburgh College of Art, Scotland. Born in East Berlin, she first trained as a tailor for women's clothing and later worked in the costume departments of various theatres, including the Comic Opera in Berlin, Scottish Opera, English National Opera and Opera Australia in Sydney. She is co-founder of Metacorpus, a company that aims to increase the awareness and appreciation of costume art through performance art productions. Her performances and exhibitions have taken her to Germany, Finland, Holland and Japan, along with research trips to Kyrgyzstan, Kazakhstan, China and Mongolia. www.sendler.co.uk

JESSICA HEMMINGS writes about textiles. She studied Textile Design at the Rhode Island School of Design, and Comparative Literature, Africa/Asia, at the University of London's School of Oriental and African Studies. Her PhD, University of Edinburgh, considered the role of textiles in the fiction of the late Zimbabwean author Yvonne Vera. She has taught at Central Saint Martins College of Art and Design, the Rhode Island School of Design and was a Reader in Textile Culture at the Winchester School of Art until October of 2008. She co-organised, with Linda Newington, the conference In the Loop: Knitting Past, Present and Future. She is currently Associate Director of the Centre for Visual and Cultural Studies at the Edinburgh College of Art, Scotland. www.jessicahemmings.com

KIRSTY ROBERTSON is a Professor of Contemporary Art and Museum Studies at the University of Western Ontario in Canada. She recently completed a SSHRC postdoctoral fellowship in the Department of Visual Arts and the Constance Howard Research Centre in Textiles at Goldsmiths College, University of London. Robertson's postdoctoral work focuses on the study of wearable technologies, immersive environments and the potential overlap/s between textiles and technologies. At present she is working on her book *Tear Gas Epiphanies: New Economies of Protest, Vision and Culture in Canada*.

DEIRDRE NELSON is an artist working in Glasgow. She completed an MPhil at the Glasgow School of Art and has pursued a parallel career in creating work for exhibition/ commission and teaching. Her textile work employs a variety of techniques and materials that fuse traditional textile skills with contemporary reinterpretation through photography and digital manipulation. Recent exhibitions include Unexpected Guests: Homes of Yesteryear, Design of Today at the Poldi Pessoli Museum, Milan, and the Artists Object Project at the Museum of Wales. She has been involved in many residencies in a variety of locations from the Outer Hebrides to Western Australia. www.deirdre-nelson.com

LIZ COLLINS is a designer and artist who specialises in knitwear, and is known internationally for her groundbreaking clothing, textiles, and installations made with manually operated knitting machines. She collaborates with other fashion designers, has an ongoing multi-media performance and installation project called *KNITTING NATION*, and teaches at Rhode Island School of Design, where she received an MFA in 1999. Collins was awarded an esteemed Target Fellowship in Crafts from United States Artists in 2006 and is currently a member of the Council of Fashion Designers of America. www.lizcollins.com

SOPHIE HORTON studied for her BA and MA at Goldsmiths, University of London. She was awarded the Unilever Award for Best Work at the London Open Biennial exhibition in 1995 and a London Arts Board Award to Individual Artists in 1998. Selected residencies include: Textile Residency, Australia National University, Canberra in 2007 and Safle, Ruthin Craft Centre in 2009. Selected solo shows include: Thames, Battersea Arts Centre, London in 1999; University of Columbus, Georgia, United States in 2003; Ban Her, Ruthin Gaol, Wales in 2009; and Hanging Out, Ruthin Craft Centre, Wales in 2009. She is an Associate Lecturer at Byam Shaw School of Art, University of the Arts London. www.sophiehorton.org

LYCIA TROUTON lectures in art and design history and theory at The Academy of Visual and Performing Arts, University of Tasmania, Launceston. Trouton was born in Belfast, Northern Ireland and grew up in Vancouver, Canada. She completed her MFA in Sculpture at Cranbrook Academy of Art, United States. Thereafter, she spent a decade working as a site-specific sculptor before moving to Australia for her Doctorate at the University of Wollongong, with an Australian Research Council Research Assistantship on "Fabric(ation)s of the Postcolonial". She subsequently lectured in Darwin and Adelaide before moving to Tasmania in 2009. Trouton has exhibited, produced community-based and/or public art commissions and attended residencies in Canada, US, Australia, UK and Asia. www.lyciatrouton.com

LACEY JANE ROBERTS holds an MFA in Fine Arts and an MA in Visual and Critical Studies from the California College of the Arts. She completed a BA in Studio Art and a BA in English from the University of Vermont. Her writing can be found in the forthcoming anthology *Extra/Ordinary: Craft Culture in Contemporary Art* published by Duke University Press. She currently serves as the co-chair of the Queer Caucus for Art, an affiliate of the College Art Association. Lacey Jane was the past recipient a 2008 Searchlight Artist Award from the American Craft Council and is a 2009 Artist-in-Residence at The Museum of Arts and Design in New York City and at Leake and Watts, a non-profit in The Bronx. www.laceyjaneroberts.com

SANDY BLACK is Professor of Fashion & Textile Design & Technology at London College of Fashion, University of the Arts. Her interests lie at the intersection of disciplines, including design, art, technology, science and mathematics, and the important role of design in sustainable futures. In 2005 she developed the Interrogating Fashion network for the discussion of key issues in fashion from which have developed collaborative research projects, events, and a new journal, *Fashion Practice:Design, Creative Process and the Fashion Industry*. She has contributed designs and articles to many publications and books on knitwear and textiles including *Wild Knitting*, 1978, *The Knitwear Revolution*, 1983, by Suzy Menkes and *Rowan's Summer and Winter Knitting*, 1987. She is the author of *Original Knitting*, 1987, *The New Knitting*, 2000, *Knitwear in Fashion*, 2002, *Fashioning Fabrics*, 2006, and *Eco Chic: the Fashion Paradox*, 2008.

ANNIE SHAW has worked as a menswear and knitwear designer based in London and the Far East for branded labels including Sabre, Aitch, Best Direction, Easy and Gabicci. She is currently a Senior Lecturer in Fashion/Knit for BA (Hons) Fashion, Textiles & Textile Design for Fashion and completed her PhD "Crafting the Technological: Ganseys and WholeGarment® Knitting" in 2009 at Manchester Metropolitan University.

AMY TWIGGER HOLROYD is the designer and sole proprietor of Keep & Share. After graduating from Manchester Metropolitan University with a degree in Fashion Design with Technology, Amy completed an MA in European Fashion and Textile Design, based jointly at the Winchester School of Art, Hogeschool voor de Kunsten Utrecht and Institut Français de la Mode, Paris, in 2003. Amy's interest in sustainable fashion design dates back to her MA, where she developed the concept for Keep & Share. Since launching the label in August 2004, she has sought to put her theoretical ideas into practice. www.keepandshare.co.uk

RACHEL BETH EGENHOEFER is an artist, designer, writer, and professor. Her work explores the intersections between textiles, technology and the body, on historical, constructional and conceptual levels. She was an MFA Fellow at the University of California, San Diego where she also was a graduate researcher at UCSD's Center for Research and Computing in the Arts (CRCA). Her work has been included in major exhibitions such as the Options 2002 Biennial in Washington DC, the 2003 Boston Cyber Arts Festival, ISEA 2004 in Tallinn Estonia, La Noche en Blanco in Madrid, The Corcoran Gallery of Art, The Institute for Contemporary Art (ICA) London, The Banff Centre for the Arts, The Lighthouse in Brighton, and others. Egenhoefer is currently an Assistant Professor of Design in the Department of Art + Architecture at the University of San Francisco. www.rachelbeth.net

KNOWLEDGEMENTS

Jessica Hemmings wishes to thank: The University of Southampton, The Edinburgh College of Art and the Pasold Research Fund who provided generous funding for the creation of this publication. The University of Southampton and the Pasold Research Fund also provided support of the conference In the Loop: Knitting Past, Present and Future, held at the Winchester School of Art from 15–17 July 2008. For funding Freddie Robins' *The Perfect* knitted sculpture for public exhibition, The Arts and Humanities Research Council (AHRC) and the Royal College of Art, Research Development Fund. An earlier version of Jo Turney's "Spinning Straw into Gold: the 'new' woman in contemporary knit lit" appears in *The Culture of Knitting*, reprinted here with the kind permission of Berg Publishers, an imprint of A&C Black Publishers Ltd. Final thanks are reserved for Mark Brown of the University of Southampton Library, whose encouragement proved invaluable to Linda Newington and I, particularly in the early stages of imagining this project.

JESSICA HEMMINGS

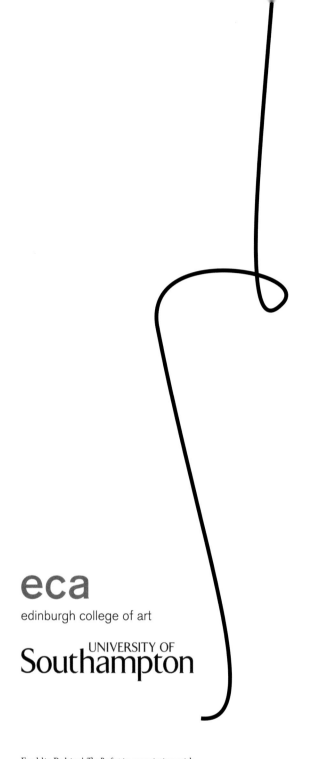

Designed by Johanna Bonnevier and Rachel Pfleger @ bdp

Black Dog Publishing Limited
10A Acton Street
London
WC1X 9NG

t.   +44 (0)207 713 5097
f.   +44 (0)207 713 8682
e.   info@blackdogonline.com

All opinions expressed within this publication are those of the author and not necessarily of the publisher.

British Library Cataloguing-in-Publication Data.
A CIP record for this book is available from the British Library.

ISBN   978 1 906155 96 4

Black Dog Publishing is an environmentally responsible company. *In the Loop: Knitting Now* is printed on an FSC certified paper. Printed in Malta by Melita Press.

cover image FREDDIE ROBINS AND CELIA PYM, *The Imperfect*, 2008. Machine knitted and hand darned wool, 160 x 50 x 50 cm. Produced through support from the Arts and Humanities Research Council (AHRC). Photograph by Celia Pym.

eca
edinburgh college of art

UNIVERSITY OF
Southampton

Freddie Robins' *The Perfect* in association with:

Royal College of Art
Postgraduate Art & Design

Arts & Humanities
Research Council

architecture art design
fashion history photography
theory and things

www.blackdogonline.com